THE THRIVING ARTISTS

Joe Abraham and Christine Negherbon

Printed in the United States of America
First Printing, 2013

ISBN: 978-1-61927-509-6

www.TheThrivingArtists.com

CONTENTS

ACKNOWLEDGMENTS

We would like to say a most sincere thank you to...

Sue Gilad for helping us move forward, Adam Vargas for artwork, Kristin Maloney for transcribing, Tracy Rosten for being our "audience," Bonnie Kole for your work and awesome pep talks that kept us going, Jonathan Flom for inspiring us with your books and giving us a platform, Career Transitions for Dancers for a wonderful grant, Matt, Kirstin, Cameron, Jillanne, Beth, Brooke, Tiffany, and Amanda for all of your interviews, Paula Currall for a final cleaning, Leslie Becker for the best advice ever (because you've been there before), and most certainly a huge thank you to every teacher we ever had. Above all, we give the biggest thanks to our parents who gave us deep roots, huge wings, and the courage to make our dreams come true...we love you.

LETTER FROM THE EDITOR

By Bonnie Kole

When Joe and Christine asked me to serve as their editor for The Thriving Artist, I enthusiastically accepted and set about the task. I had no idea that my entire mindset about career management and personal financial management would be changed forever…and I am not even an artist!

As I edited page after page, I found myself having many "Gee whiz, who knew?" moments and before the end of the first chapter, I was hooked on becoming a *thriving* individual in my professional life and my personal finances. I was able to embrace the mindset that Joe and Christine described (and live by) because it was so totally based in common sense. I also knew that if Joe and Christine could make this work in the tentative world of show business, then anyone could make this work in any field of endeavor.

The notion that really appealed to me was to pay yourself first. I like the fact that to thrive, you have to really put the need for instant gratification in perspective. Sure, we all find ourselves wanting something when we want it, but at what price to the important goals? Everything has a price, and to thrive, you have to ask yourself if the price today is worth your future success tomorrow. This is common sense, it is brilliant, and it is reinforced throughout these pages.

Joe and Christine are thriving. They set short and long-term goals, and consistently "check in" with these goals when deciding to accept a project, manage their money, make sure there is a profit in every job, and to seriously weigh the benefits of renting versus buying real estate; and that is just for openers. As thriving artists, Joe and Christine have taken a hard look at the realities of their chosen profession (and since performing is what they love and are incredibly great at it) decided what they needed to do to support the "tentativeness" of show business. They assessed their other marketable skills, and used those skills to earn money when performing opportunities were not there. Joe and Christine ask their readers to think outside of the box; for example, as dancers, they absolutely needed to continually take classes and that can be costly. What to do? Our thriving artists offered to clean the dance studio in exchange for dance lessons. This was a common sense solution, without a doubt. I thought about this, and when my husband and I needed to update our wills, I bartered educational consulting services for legal services with a friend of mine who is an attorney. I never would have thought to barter services, had it not been for Joe and Christine's Thriving Artists mindset.

Joe and Christine know that in order to thrive, every business decision, every financial decision must be in alignment with the goals that are set; and while this is more common sense, I found myself looking at my goals and the decisions (financial especially) I was making. I had another "Gee whiz, who knew?" moment, because my goals and decisions were out of sync. I decided right then and there to *thrive* and although changing a mindset that has been with me nearly forty years was hard, I am seeing the benefits each and every day. I may not be out of the financial woods yet, but each day I check in with my goals and decisions; and I am discovering that I am on my way to a better financial future *and* I have more projects happening than ever before.

Joe and Christine are not making any promises or giving you any guarantees; rather, they are asking you, the reader, to hold your dreams up to the light and decide if the images are pretty enough to work hard and make those dreams a reality. The only way to thrive is to *decide* to thrive, and if you make that decision, then take Joe and Christine on the journey with you; they know the route and will point out all of sites to see and places to avoid.

Thriving is a great journey, and a great destination.

FOREWORD

By Jonathan Flom

You have made a very shrewd decision in picking up this book and giving it a read. You would be wiser yet to read this with a highlighter and a notepad (or iPad, as the case may be!) because you will want to take copious notes and review Joe and Christine's advice often. I have known Joe since we were freshman at Penn State together, in a budding musical theatre program; and I can attest to the fact that this man has been a goal-setter and an against-all-odds achiever since he came out of high school. What I have seen this "power couple" (as I call them) accomplish within the industry of show business—and in their life outside of the biz—is nothing short of remarkable and inspiring, and I am so glad that they finally put their story and their guiding principles down in writing to share with the world, because really, we deserve it!

Reading this book is your first step toward empowerment. Joe and Christine are offering not just dry, technical council, but a way of life that, if followed, will keep you healthy and fulfilled. It's unfortunate that most college programs don't teach this stuff, but now you have it laid out for you in manageable terms. It's time to ask yourself what is your personal vision of success. It's time to define it for yourself and to forget about what society or friends and family have deemed successful. Figure out what you really want out of life, and then use this book to guide you towards reaching your personal goals. If you can dream it, you can achieve it. But believe me, it will take a lot of perseverance and hard work on your part. So if you are truly determined and ready to put in the work, turn the page and begin a very exciting journey that far too few artists choose to take. Dare to be one of the rare few who chooses the path of Thriving.

Jonathan Flom
Author, *Act Like It's Your Business* & *Get the Callback*
Musical Theatre Program Coordinator, Shenandoah Conservatory
www.jonathanflom.com

PREFACE

By Sue Gilad

Clever you to have found your way to Joe Abraham and Christine Negherbon. You just discovered a shortcut to success and fulfillment—by following those who have created a full and thriving life, not just in their careers but in every aspect of being.

You already know about their achievements as individuals: Joe chased his Broadway dreams all the way to *The Little Mermaid* and *Hairspray*, and then, constantly moving forward, headed to Los Angeles to pursue his active TV and film career. During the writing of this book, Joe was booking gigs on TV's *Touch* as well as film leads.

Christine made waves on the national tour of *My Fair Lady*, produced by Cameron Mackintosh, and starred as Peggy Sawyer in the European tour of *42nd Street*. Her choreography has been mounted across the country in *Crazy For You*, *West Side Story*, *The World Goes Round*, and *Cabaret*. If you live on the Left Coast you may have caught Christine tearing up the boards in *CATS* at Sacramento Music Circus.

Yet that is just the beginning of the story. Most artists would be content with that level of professional success—and perhaps have a "survival" job between gigs to keep the funds flowing. But Joe and Christine, using the same development skills they bring to every audition, created and continue to create business ventures that complement their livelihoods. Joe's website development company provides actors and businesses with a fully integrated platform—offering unlimited reach and impact. Christine's custom cosmetics company turns performers into the physical embodiment of the role. Together Christine and Joe have invested in real estate and internet franchises. Best of all, Joe and Christine are delighted to share their vast stores of knowledge with you. (Lucky you.)

What you hold in your hands is not just a primer for professional fulfillment. Not simply a guide to financial wealth creation. Not merely a channel for creating your own opportunity and destiny. It is a story of happiness and how to achieve it. Joe and Christine are recognized in several realms—performance, business, coaching and mentoring. But everyone who is fortunate enough to be close to

Christine and Joe personally knows that their proudest achievements are as a loving couple and best parents ever to their son Cole. The home they have created is warm and inviting. Their positive energy and dedicated focus on building a life of joy and fun is the most inspiring element to witness.

If you are committed to your own success, and creating magic while you smell the roses along the way, you have found the couple who blazed the path for you…and then generously shared all those gifts, in the secrets you will find within. Savor every page, and then go out and DO—as Christine and Joe would want you to. Bravo.

To every success,
Sue Gilad
Author, *The Real Estate Millionaire* and
Copyediting and Proofreading for Dummies

INTRODUCTION

"A mighty flame followeth a tiny spark."
- Dante

"May this book be that spark in your life."
– Joe and Christine

You are an artist. Congratulations! You have made a huge commitment to yourself and your art. You have chosen a profession that requires putting yourself, your heart, and your soul out there…on the line, every day. You are truly one of the bravest beings on the planet, and never let anyone discourage you or tell you that your dreams cannot come true. We mean that with the utmost sincerity, because *we are you*. Our chosen art is acting both on stage and on camera and what we say will speak from our experiences in these art forms. However, this book is for *all artists*, everywhere.

We are two people who came from small towns in Pennsylvania, followed our dreams, and have the privilege of living them every day. We have waited in lines at chorus calls and have gotten up before dawn to sign in for an EPA (Equity Principal Audition—more on this later). We have worked in nearly every type of performing venue, including theme parks, regional theatres, dinner theatres, cruise ships, industrials, multiple tours of the U.S. and Europe, and Broadway for over thirty-two years collectively. We have also tended bar, waited tables, managed restaurants, catered, distributed fliers on the street, painted apartments for voice lessons, cleaned dance studios to take class at a discount, worked with a temp agency, set up and tore down trade shows… you name it, we probably did it. We have worked, sweated, and stayed focused, even in the face of being rejected time and again. Because of the principles and valuable experiences we outline here, we continue to *thrive* every day.

You can too!

However, we have noticed over the years that there is a negative sentiment (attitude) within the artistic community, the sentiment of being a starving artist. This book is all about awareness and education and empowerment. So first we must be aware in order to make a change. With that being said, wherever you are in your artistic and financial journey, consider the following scenarios and decide if any (or all) of them sound familiar.

Scenario 1: You live in New York City (or any city) where you have a survival job that barely covers rent and expenses; *and* after working that survival job, you end your day by going out to bars where you know the bartender, and you get free drinks. You audition and take class sporadically, often *prying* yourself out of bed to get there because you closed the restaurant/bar somewhere between 2 and 4 am. You live this way because you are young, talented, and fabulous! **You are a Starving Artist.**

Scenario 2: You live for your *art*. You think an artist who makes a lot of money, is "selling out." You would much rather do evocative, heart-wrenching pieces for little or no money than go into another production of *Noises Off* in Smalltown, USA. A job comes along and it brings you twelve weeks of work, some savings in the bank, and your health insurance. Yes! The twelve weeks have passed, the run is over, your contract is over, and your *first* call is to the unemployment office. The savings you recently earned are dwindling, since you have been living off these funds for the past few weeks. You are heading right back in the direction described in Scenario 1. **You are a Starving Artist.**

Scenario 3: Broadway calls and your dream has come true! You have worked hard, and it is everything you hoped it would be. You are making more money than ever and you have every reason to celebrate! Right on the heels of signing your Broadway contract you *also* sign a lease on a new and fabulous midtown studio apartment. You are now frequenting all the hottest bars and clubs in Manhattan. You buy the latest tech gadget and a huge flat-screen TV. Your name is on Playbill.com. You are on an original cast recording, and you have performed on "The View," "GMA" and the like. Then, the reviews come out and your closing notice goes up. You don't know how you are going to pay next month's rent. Now what? Will it be back to the life in Scenario 1? **You are a Starving Artist.** You get the idea.

We are here to tell you that *you can live the life you have dreamed about.* You can do provocative, heart-wrenching art. You can live in Midtown, Weho, or any trendy neighborhood you wish. You can be the artist you envision. You can afford it, *if you are determined not to be a starving artist.*

We take issue with the notion of a "starving" artist (and you should too), because it is not a condition or a lifestyle, but a *mindset.* All artists should be *thriving* because artists are some of the most intelligent, talented, and vibrant beings on the planet.

Artists have the power to create living, breathing art that moves people to laughter and tears. We bring joy to countless people and truly make this world a better place. In many areas of life, artists can look beyond the obvious, so how can we often be so uninformed and unaware about money and it's management?

There is no reason why you cannot have the apartment, the car, the family, *and* your art. You can have it all, and we can show you a way.

We are not former actors who are now coaches or armchair critics. We are artists who started from nothing, and are thriving every day in a career we love. We can show you a way, because we are *still successfully in the game.*

So, Joe and Christine, why did you write this book?

We wrote this book quite simply because we had to. It was bursting out of us. Once we realized the state of our beloved artists community, and once we realized how much we have to share, it was just a matter of time until we finished this labor of love that you are now reading.

Our mission is to joyously promote living the life of a *Thriving Artist,* and in the process completely eradicate the term "starving artist" from our vocabulary and mindset. We wrote this book to show you how to *thrive* in every aspect of your artistic career as well as in your financial life. Hearing our fellow actors and artists saying, "I'm broke" as they just came off a huge summer contract or (worse yet) a Broadway contract was a major cause for concern.

This book will shine a light on some entrenched myths that being an artist somehow equates to being a disempowered, non-business minded, horrible money manager who is always sitting around waiting for the telephone to ring. We do not and we will not buy into that perception. Ever.

We are here to change that perception and ultimately *transform* your mindset about what it means to live the life of an artist; and it all begins with a *choice*…

Starve or Thrive?

Thriving: (adjective) Booming: very lively and profitable. Flourishing: having or showing vigorous life. Doing well. Syn: prospering, prosperous, roaring

Starving: (adjective) Dying of hunger, deprived of nourishment, causing to capitulate by or as if by depriving of nourishment. Syn: very hungry, ravenous, famished.

"It is in your moments of decision that your
destiny is shaped."
- Anthony Robbins

THRIVING ARTIST'S CHOICE
We choose our thoughts every minute of every day, whether we are conscious of it or not. Throughout this book, we are going to bring a *focused* awareness to this process of choice. We want to emphasize that it is, always has been, and always will be your choice. What you believe and the actions you take based on those beliefs are 100 percent up to you, so it is time to take control of that process starting right now.

Think about creating your life and career as an artist, and then read the two thought choices below:

Thriving Thought: *"I have a positive, empowered, and forward-thinking mindset in the core of my being. My life is 100 percent up to me and I am capable of more than I ever thought possible. I create it. I take action on it. I live it every day."*

Starving Thought: *"I take life and my career as it comes. I wait and see what's out there and hope that something good comes my way. This business is hard, and I don't know exactly how I'm gonna make it, but I sure hope I do."*

Take a moment and consider the *Thriving Thought* and the *Starving Thought*; then take a pen and circle the thought that you will play over and over in your mind while you build your life and career as an artist. Congratulations. This is the first step.

> "We are what we think. All that we are arises with our thoughts. With our thoughts, we make our world."
> **- Buddha**

Chapter 1 - A New Paradigm

It's about an internal shift. A conscious adjustment that will enable you to achieve what you want to achieve because you will be holding yourself in an empowering context. You have to "be it before you see it" and it's about being a Thriving Artist versus a starving artist. The difference lies *within you,* and it has nothing to do with whether or not you are working/getting paid through your art. You may be surprised to hear that, but it is true. We have worked with many people on Broadway and around the country, and though they were working steadily and making lots of money, they were still "starving artists." We know Tony Award® winners who, years later, are now "starving."

PAUSE RIGHT NOW.

Take a moment and seriously think about what you just read. Consider the two mindsets that emerge within you. You now have to make a choice about your life, your career, and your finances.

Do you choose, as of this moment, to be done with making excuses and blaming everything around you for what you don't have? Are you ready to take responsibility for every aspect of your life, career, and finances, and *make* them great?

Are you ready to *be* a Thriving Artist?

Or are you comfortable where you are? Are you satisfied with what gets tossed your way in the whirlwind of life? Are you content to sit by the phone waiting for it to ring, and when it doesn't, spend your time talking about all the reasons why that silent phone is not your fault? Are you OK with being a starving artist?

Choose.

If you choose the latter, please close this book now. We can do nothing to help you. However, if you chose the former, it means that you are ready to make huge things happen!

Congratulations! You have chosen to be a Thriving Artist!

It really is that simple, and it's why we have you choose at the beginning. Your context for your life determines the content of your life. In other words, you will get a life full of things that resonate with *what you say you are*. For example, if you look at yourself like a coffee mug (context), most likely coffee (content) will come your way. Now let's say you want champagne in your life, but you haven't shifted your context from that of a coffee mug to a champagne flute. Well, champagne doesn't inherently go in a coffee mug...never has and never will. You can go to France and learn all there is to know about champagne, but at the end of the day champagne goes in the flute, not the mug. If your context says you are one thing (either consciously or unconsciously) but you are always yearning for different content than what you have, then it's time to transform and be the thing that's in line with what you want. The quote from Anthony Robbins says, "If you do what you've always done, you'll get what you've always gotten." We like to say, "If you BE who you've always been, you'll get what you've always gotten." Because what's being done isn't quite as important as *who's doing it*. Focus on the who, and you won't be a coffee mug in search of champagne. If you want an artistic career bursting with fulfillment and financial abundance, *then you have to BE a Thriving Artist*. And if you are still reading this, you've made the right choice!

Now, here is the reality check and there is absolutely no way around it: If you can't get up every morning and look yourself in the mirror and go to work, you're going to have a very hard time building the career and life of your dreams.

Being a Thriving Artist is like being a professional athlete. You have to be at the top of your game to compete. Does that mean that everyone on Broadway is the best actor, singer, or dancer? No. Does that mean famous people in other art forms are all the very best at what they do? No. We all know people who have landed a Broadway show while we can't imagine who on earth would cast them. However, we are not talking about one show or one piece of art; we are talking about a career. We want you to have many shows, films, gallery presentations etc. We want you to be able to buy the house when you are ready and to have kids when the time is right. Ultimately, we want consistently working artists who simultaneously put time and energy into empowering their lives and managing their finances. We never want to hear the term "starving artist" again. It's a cop-out. Period.

Here you'll find systems, techniques, advice, personal stories, interviews, practical knowledge, and even some concepts that may take a minute to sink in. All will help you be the best Thriving Artist you can be.

As with any book like this, you may not agree with everything we say. Some of it may even agitate you a little. To that we lovingly say…get over it. We're not here to coddle you and tell you it's going to be easy. Let's face it; if it were easy, everyone would be doing it.

Our sincerest hope is that you find what you read here useful in all areas of your life, not just your artistic career.

We thank you again for your time and energy in reading this book. We are, and always will be, on your side and rooting for you every step of the way.

Now let's get to work!

THRIVING ARTISTS FOCUSES

We have identified five focus areas, each covered in the following chapters, in which any artist (no matter what status or number of years in the business) needs to direct his or her time, and energy. Once we have covered these areas in detail, you will have a clear and structured way of categorizing every action you take and its relevance to your career. If you are not seeing the results you want, we can all but guarantee that the work you need to do falls into one of these areas:

1. FOCUS ON YOU: Your head, your heart, and getting congruent

2. FOCUS ON GOALS: Getting specific about what you want, when you want it, and how to make it happen

3. FOCUS ON SEEING AND BEING SEEN: Auditioning, marketing, and branding

4. FOCUS ON RELATIONSHIPS: Building your network successfully

5. FOCUS ON FINANCES: Money management and asset creation

Chapter 2 – Focus On: You
Your head, your heart, and getting congruent.

When you look in the mirror, what do you see?

How you view yourself and your career are the most important things to consider when thinking like a Thriving Artist; and it's why we begin with these points of awareness. It is one thing to choose to be a Thriving Artist; we are now going to give you the tools to make that decision manifest into your reality. In this section we will also take a look at the types of knowledge and information needed - about yourself and your career - that will enable you to venture into your artistic achievement in an empowered way.

Let's begin with the importance of how you view yourself and what influences that perspective the most.

How you do *anything* is how you do *everything*. It all stems from your attitude. But what are the pieces of the puzzle that fit together to form your attitude about something? What are the steps you always use in your decision-making process? We discovered something we call the Creation Cycle: the process by which we as humans create anything and everything. (Note: We are not implying any sort of religious meaning when we use the term Creation Cycle. We are simply giving the process of manifestation an easy name for reference). The Creation Cycle looks like this:

$$\text{Thoughts} \rightarrow \text{Feelings} \rightarrow \text{Actions} \rightarrow \text{Results}$$

THOUGHTS
We all have a million voices in our head, and we generically call them our thoughts. These thoughts are the ongoing conversations we have with ourselves that tell us where to go and what to do. They spring from three areas: conscious intake of information, environment, and programming. (So once a decision is made to do something, it becomes a matter of gathering the relevant information, which supports those internal conversations.)

When you have a goal, you consciously gather information about it through books, seminars, classes, conversations with friends, etc., all of which can help you move forward. Be mindful of what you are gathering and make sure it will help propel you in the direction of your goal.

An equally important and often overlooked element that affects your thoughts is your environment. For example, are the five people closest to you succeeding in their art? Are they succeeding financially? Do they complain about what they don't have, or do they work to create what they need? How do they affect you? Do they encourage your growth artistically? Do they push you to your limits or let you get away with less than your best? You must evaluate whether you are in the most supportive environment or not, because it directly impacts your thoughts.

The last area that affects your thoughts, a combination of the previous two, is your "programming." For a moment, let's look at your brain like a computer.

It is widely accepted that the human brain is the most powerful super computer on the planet and there is no limit to its learning capacity. In other words, your brain will never be full. Some scientists calculate that our brains can store an estimated 2.5 million gigabytes of information. That fact should make you pause in awe for just a moment. The sheer magnitude of the brain's capacity to store information is truly incredible, but we can also *create* new ideas from the stored information that we already have! We can connect different dots and cross-pollinate information, we can dream, and we can imagine. However, there is a catch. In all its glory, the human brain, like any computer, does what it is *programmed* to do. Here is the "aha" moment: *You* are that programmer! *You* are in control of what goes in, and in turn, what comes out. You need to be keenly aware that you are always 100 percent in charge of what *you allow* into your brain. We are emphatically saying "quality in, quality out"; and conversely, "garbage in, garbage out." Once you wake up to that fact, there is no going back to sleep. You are responsible from that moment on. Understanding this basic reality is vitally important to being a Thriving Artist.

You must recognize there may be some programs in your brain that you weren't conscious of when they were being created; however, as of this moment, you now have the *awareness* to keep them, change them, or delete them altogether. The neural pathways in your brain are much like tracks that wagon wheels create on a dirt road. The more a certain path is used, the easier and more habitual it becomes to take that same path or follow a certain program. You can *always* create a new trail or a new program. *You are in the driver's seat.*

> ## "Man's mind stretched to a new idea never goes back to its original dimensions."
> ### *- Oliver Wendell Holmes*

Programs have all been learned at some point throughout your life, and that means they can be unlearned if they are not useful. A program is just a bit of information you absorbed somewhere and is now a thought that plays on constant repeat inside your head. When that program (thought) gets repeated often enough, it leads to our next step in the Creation Cycle.

FEELINGS
Several layers make up your emotions. Once enough information comes in, and your thoughts are played over and over again, these thoughts become entrenched and form a *belief*. A belief is like a net that is cast over your brain and acts like a filter for all the information you come in contact with every day.

A belief is also like a personal fact that you hold about yourself or the world. On any given day, there is a massive amount of information coming at you, and the filter of your beliefs tells you how you feel about that information and where you will file it. Your beliefs also act like little radio towers that are continuously seeking out information on their "frequency"; that "frequency" validates the existence of your beliefs and keep them entrenched in your brain.

For example, if you hold the belief that traffic is *always* terrible, more than likely, you will always disregard the times when traffic was great, because it doesn't validate your belief and you are not mentally programmed to accept a good day of traffic as the norm. You might say, "The good traffic was a fluke." The same rules apply when you go on an audition. You go in, you do wonderfully, and it validates your belief that you are great at auditioning. Even if you didn't nail your performance, chances are you will find something that you *did* do well and hold on to it. You will not dwell on the things that went wrong and beat yourself up over it.

Conversely, if you have the belief that you *aren't* good at auditions...the information from the experience will pass through your filters, you will delete anything good that happened, and you'll validate the belief that you are awful at auditions. Makes sense, right? Pause for a moment and consider your beliefs about yourself, your art, and your finances. Are they empowering or disempowering? Are they serving your success? Think back to your most recent audition or performance and see how your beliefs affected your interpretation of the experience.

> **"Beliefs have the power to create and the power to destroy. Human beings have the awesome ability to take any experience of their lives and create a meaning that disempowers them or one that can literally save their lives."**
> **– Anthony Robbins**

Beliefs are dependent on internalized support. Because it isn't happening on a conscious level, most people are unaware of the process. The strength of any belief depends on how much support it has. Think of it like a building made entirely of bricks. The more bricks that have been laid in place (thoughts/experiences), the bigger and stronger that building will become (belief). To create a new belief about ourselves, we just have to have an empowering thought and repeat that thought over and over again. The repetitious thought we play in our heads also tunes our "internal radio tower" to seek out and remember experiences in line with that new thought. Those validating experiences are like the bricks creating the building, and each time the thought plays, and we have an experience in line with that thought, we lay another brick to support that new belief.

Joe: I used to be terrible at remembering people's names - I mean absolutely awful. I would ask someone's name and then forget it as soon as they were finished saying it. So one day I got mad enough and decided to change it. I needed to create a new belief. I told myself, "I'm getting better at remembering names." I said it that way, because I knew that my brain would accept it. If I had said, "I'm great at remembering names" my brain would have rejected it as something that was completely opposite the norm. I kept saying that to myself over and over and over, and I would practice with everyone I met. If I quickly forgot a name, I would just own up to it and ask again, telling them I was working on getting better with names. Now, a few *years later, I can honestly say I am pretty close to being a "name ninja"! I have made it a game for myself and every time I get it right, I win. I have successfully trans-formed a negative belief, simply by stating the <u>positive</u> opposite of what I wanted to change in a way that my brain would accept. Then I looked for instances when I got it right in order to validate and strengthen that new belief.*

You are 100 percent capable of *changing anything you want* about your beliefs.

You just have to *do* it.

Our network of beliefs is what ultimately determines our feelings and attitudes about something, and this is the crossroad when most people are aware, or at least partially aware, of themselves and their beliefs. Try the following exercise:

Using your first reaction, complete each sentence. Be honest here.

My art is…

Auditions are…

Networking is…

Selling is…

Working out is…

How did you complete each sentence? Did you complete each sentence in a positive or negative light? Was your answer empowering or disempowering? What do your responses say about your beliefs?

This exercise asked you to work on surface information and your beliefs; however, in order to make real change, you need to go deeper. Most people try to change their attitude and feelings without working on anything below the surface, and then they wonder why there was no lasting change. So look at any negative answers again and reverse engineer them. What thoughts, information, and environmental circumstances do you have surrounding that topic? What programs (information loops) have been created so far? What beliefs were born of these programs? How does that belief affect you on a gut emotional level when considering the topics above? If your answers were negative, how can you make them positive? Rewrite them now in an empowering way that will tune your radio tower to seek out new information.

My art is…

Auditions are…

Networking is…

Selling is…

Working out is…

Your feelings are the surface manifestation of everything beneath them (thoughts, programming, beliefs, etc.). Those feelings are what people listen to when it comes time to do or not do something. You tend to do something, because *you feel* like it, or on the flip side, you don't do something, because *you don't feel* like it.

This now leads us to the next step in the Creation Cycle, which is the bridge between your inner world and your outer world.

ACTIONS

Actions are the precursor to any result, but they come at the end of a chain of internal events. What determines your success or failure in anything is what *you choose to do*! Yet the key to succeeding in anything lies beneath the surface.

> "Deep within man dwell those slumbering powers;
> powers that would astonish him, that he never dreamed
> of possessing; forces that would revolutionize his life if
> aroused and put into action."
> **– Orison Swett Marden**

You don't build a house on quicksand, nor do you take action to achieve your dreams with a head full of bad wiring. It is all internal. Clearly, you have to *take action* to get anything accomplished. If you want to be the best of the best in what you do, you'll have to take *massive action* to make that happen. Now with awareness and control over your thoughts and emotions, you can also take *inspired* action. Who you are being, and the energy you bring to that action, is crucial in influencing the last part of the Creation Cycle.

RESULTS
Results are the physical manifestation of steps One through Three in the Creation Cycle. It is extremely important that we do not judge our results. It may be difficult, but we have to resist the urge to judge. Most of the time, people will have an opinion on the results of an action, saying it was "good" or "bad" that "I was great" or "I was terrible." You must not judge!

From the moment a result is produced, a new Creation Cycle has begun. Most of the time, people will judge their results through a veil of emotions and beliefs without ever being aware of the useful information they may be missing. That overlooked information is critical to further success!

The best way to look at results is to do so with absolutely no emotional judgment or attachment whatsoever. Look at the results and determine whether your actions were effective or ineffective in bringing about your desired result.

"There is no failure, only feedback."
– Joe & Christine

Simply put, either something worked or it didn't. Did your actions get you closer to your goal? If so, that's great. If not, so be it. There is no need to get upset about it. Get over it. Move on. We understand that emotions will flow through your mind (and body), but you can't let them take over and become "fact." Let the emotion come and go just like the weather. Learn, adjust, and keep going. Take Thomas Edison for example. It took him more than 9,000 attempts before he created a light bulb that would burn for 1,500 hours. It is guaranteed he felt a lot of frustration, but those feelings never stopped him. It may seem counterintuitive to approach your artistic career like a scientist, but it works!

Thriving Thought: If you want to change your results, you must first consciously change your intake of information, thoughts, emotions, and actions!

An example of the whole Creation Cycle might look something like this:

John Actor goes in for an audition. It doesn't go the way he wanted and he does not get a callback. John isn't very self-aware, so he beats himself up emotionally and tells himself that he is lousy at auditions. John's brain, not knowing the difference in supportive and non-supportive information (thoughts), simply logs it in and runs it on a constant loop (program). He has told himself the same thing so often that he now "knows" (belief) that he stinks at auditions. John continues to "loop" his negative belief when he is out with his actor friends; in fact, he might even talk or joke about how badly auditions go for him. A week or so goes by and he hears about another audition for a show he would love to do. He begrudgingly (attitude) buys the trade newspaper and sees that it is indeed a perfect part for him, but as soon as he reads it John gets a knot in his stomach (feelings) because, of course, he will have to audition. Determined to press on, he does his best to prepare, although he really doesn't feel like it (feelings). He does just enough (action), but when his friends call him up to go play cards the night before his audition, instead of staying in and working, he goes out (action), because working on his material isn't all that much fun for him anyway (attitude). The day of the audition arrives and, as always, he is nervous. John tells himself that he has done enough, but when he goes into the room, his nerves take over and he does just OK. He doesn't forget any of his lines, but he also doesn't nail it like he knew he could have. Once again, our friend John walks out of the room beating himself up (maybe even worse this time) and the entire Cycle begins all over again.

Think about John's input and output. Were his results a surprise based upon his internal life and the actions he chose?

Joe: I recently had an audition where the exact opposite of the above example happened to me. I was called in for a co-starring role on the Fox TV show Touch *with Kiefer Sutherland. It all happened very quickly, from the time I got the audition material until I was in the room with the casting director. I had done my work and prepared to the very best of my ability. I read once, she gave me directions, and I did it one more time. That was it. I walked out of there feeling like I could have done better and wishing I had done more somehow. As soon as I realized I was going down this mental "starving artist" path I literally said out loud to myself, "Stop it!" I then asked myself, "What did I do well?" and "What did I do that represented myself in a good light?" Then I waited for an answer. I got one. I actually got several! I remembered all the things I did well and started focusing on them. Immediately I was taking control of the Creation Cycle and not allowing negative information to loop in my brain. Everything changed in an instant. Who knows if my internal journey had anything to do with it, but I ended up booking that job and working on the show for a day! Booking that first network TV show is one of my proudest moments in my career to this day. I'm telling this story not to brag, but just to show the power we have when we take ownership of our thoughts, feelings, and actions so we create space for our desired results to materialize.*

The Creation Cycle is something we must be aware of at all times, because it is always happening. Taking control of it and dictating what programming goes into your brain (thus affecting the resulting feelings and actions) can inspire and empower you to create virtually anything you want.

Quick Focal Point

One of the main components in this book is the topic of handling money while being an artist. We will cover it much more depth later, but we want to touch on it right now, while we are discussing our "inner world." The attitude *you create* about money is one of the main things you will need to look at as you continue your journey to being a Thriving Artist. We have a certain attitude toward money that has served to strengthen us as we create our lives as Thriving Artists. We hope you choose to make what you see below, or some version of it, your own.

Our attitude is this:

The moment you decide that the thing you love to do is going to be your livelihood and main source of income is the same moment when you can no longer do it solely because you love it. It must become your business, be treated like one, and you should be highly paid for it.

To some this may seem like common sense. To others it may be unsettling. You might disagree with it on some level because it may be in direct contrast with the conventional (often unconsciously learned) wisdom that if you do what you love you shouldn't make a lot of money doing it. To that idea we say, it's crap. If this concept of being highly paid and doing what you love *does* bother you, ask yourself why. Where did you learn it? How does it serve you? And why would you choose to hang on to it if it doesn't serve you and your dreams? If you think being a starving artist somehow helps the world, we recommend questioning that point of view. How does your being a poor, starving artist help other people? How does suffering needlessly help your art? We are raising these questions so you can confront some things inside that you may not have looked at in the past. We're not saying you *must* adopt our view; we are simply shining a light on the topic and letting you know you have a choice.

*Christine: We saw an example of this disposition play out in the NFL, and it was revealing how I reacted to it. While I was watching a game on television, the announcers told a story about a player who had signed with a team and was supposed to play, but was having a dispute about how much money he was going to make that year. It was the middle of the season, and he hadn't yet played in a single game. He was still in contract negotiations. At first I was annoyed with him for holding out for more money. I mean, come on, this guy had already made millions, right? What did he need more money for? And wasn't this game of football supposed to be fun? Wasn't it what he lived for and loved to do more than anything? Why all the hubbub about money? Shortly after I had my initial emotional reaction to the news, I started to use the other half of my brain - the **business** half. It was then that I was actually, in an odd way, proud of what this player was doing. That may sound surprising, but let me explain. There are three essential lessons that we can all learn from this situation, and they apply directly to our line of work as artists. This NFL player demonstrated that:*

#1 He knows what he is worth and he is willing to say no.
#2 He does not believe that he should be paid less because he is doing a job he loves.
#3 He is approaching the game like a business.

Let's look at each lesson in more detail.

Lesson #1
The first thing we can learn is that this player knows what he is worth and is willing to decline a lowball offer. He has no doubt in his abilities and knows that if he accepted less money, he would be selling himself short. He may (or may not) be a millionaire, but that does not matter. The point is you have to be aware of what the market will bear. To put it simply, if you are in demand, then you should receive compensation in line with that demand.

To some people it may seem selfish and egotistical for this man to ask for several more millions of dollars in his contract, but if his athletic talent is bringing fans to the games, and the team owners are making money off his talent, he should reap appropriate financial rewards. You can say what you like about greed or players' salaries being too high, but if the owner makes $500 million per season, and a player is asking to go from $5 million to $9 million per season because he helps lead the team to victory, you can see that it is not an outrageous request in that market.

Let's also look at his willingness to say no to performing his role as a team player. Pause and think about that for a moment. Note your reaction. What is going on inside your head? Are you amazed? Are you cheering him on? Are you angry and thinking he's foolish? Now, put yourself in a parallel situation. You are being offered a contract renewal with your long-running Broadway show. You have given 100 percent every time you walk on stage, you show up ready to work with a good attitude, and people are coming to the show to see *you*. Yet when the producers come to you with a renewal contract, it reflects a *pay cut*. They still want you to do eight shows a week, and ticket prices will be the same, but they are offering you less money to perform the same role. What do you do? The question is not simple, and before you can answer it, you need to ask yourself very seriously, "*What do I think I am worth?*" Pause for a moment and write down a number that you should get paid per week for your talent. Do this now in the space below.

My talent is worth $_____ per week/project/film/painting (insert your art form here)

Our point is that *you are only worth what you are willing to accept as payment for your talent.* You can't blame any producer for wanting to pay the least amount allowable. The producer's job is to present a quality product and provide the investors with a return. The artist's job is to know the market, know what you are worth, and be adamant about appropriate compensation; otherwise, you'll always *get* what you always *got*. Sometimes saying no can be the best thing for your career; and we know many artists who have found out what a producer was willing to pay when they were willing to walk away from the job. It cuts both ways, of course, because you could be willing to walk away, and the producer could be willing to let you go. It's a chance you may have to take if the time comes.

Lesson #2

The second thing to be learned is that the football player knows that even though he loves to play the game, it does *not* mean that he shouldn't be well paid for it. This speaks directly to your personal financial programming and is something we will explore more in the financial section of this book. For now simply note your reaction to the following statement:

"If you love what you do, you should be highly paid for it."

Do you agree or disagree with this statement? There is no wrong answer; however, from our point of view, in order to be a Thriving Artist, *you must agree with that statement*. Otherwise a part of you will always resist being paid well for doing what you love. If you think that the love of your art will always be payment enough, ask your landlord to accept a good monologue performance in lieu of the rent. Let us know how that goes for you!

Lesson #3

The final lesson to be learned here is the most important one of all. Every single one of us started performing, painting, directing, designing, etc., because we loved it. Whatever it was about doing that thing, it took us to another place and made us happier than we have ever been, and we couldn't imagine spending our lives doing anything else. True? We hope so. However, there is another consideration, something that is virtually never talked about:

Your art must become your *business*, be treated like one, and you must be highly paid for it.

You have to make a conscious shift from doing it just for the love (which hopefully never leaves you) to doing it because it also pays you. Please do not let others take advantage of the fact that you love what you do. Command their respect, and know that you are deserving of professional compensation for your efforts at all times. Let your charity work be just that, and let your professional work pay you at the highest rate possible. *Do not let the love of your art make someone else rich at your expense.*

> "Money is better than poverty, if only for financial
> reasons."
> **– Woody Allen**

With all of this in mind, let's again take a look at the professional athlete who is "playing a game for a living" and understand what we, as artists, have in common. Do we not "play" as well? We get cast in *plays*. We *play* instruments. We *play* out a scene in a film. If you ever hit a creative block, did your mentors and teachers ever tell you to just let go and…play? And now think about it: You get paid for what you do. You get paid to play. Couldn't people less fortunate say the same thing about how much *you* make? You may be "singing and dancing for a living" and from their perspective, you are highly overpaid. Believe us when we tell you that you are not. You are a working professional in a market that can bear that compensation, and you have every right to feel good about claiming it.

We can transform our entire community of artists to view their work in this way.

It starts with you.

> "Knowledge is power. Information is liberating.
> Education is the premise of progress, in every society,
> in every family."
> **– Kofi Annan**

Knowledge is the next piece of Focus On: You. There are three types of knowledge that we will now cover in detail:

1. Talent, skill, and practical knowledge
2. Book knowledge
3. Professional knowledge

1. Talent, Skill, and Practical Knowledge

Talent is something that cannot really be taught; however, it can be nurtured and developed. It is the raw material you've been given to work with. Skill is the ability to showcase or communicate that talent. If you think of it like a sculptor to clay, your talent is the clay and your skill is what you are able to sculpt with it. On your professional journey both talent and skill are required to get where you want to go. Success is achieved when you identify your artistic talents and develop the specific skills needed to share those gifts. We all know people who have been gifted from God in what they are innately able to do, yet never "made it big" because they had no skills or discipline to develop that talent. On the flip side we can all name artists who did not have the best "raw material" at the start, but who worked tirelessly at developing themselves to become huge successes in their fields.

Thriving Thought: *It's not what you have; it's what you do with what you have that counts!*

Let's take this conversation one step further and look at it in today's market. Our expertise is performing in theater and on camera, so we will use that as our example. So, what does it take to "make it" these days?

Thriving Artists: Can you dance?
You: Yes.
Thriving Artists: Good. Can you sing?
You: Absolutely!
Thriving Artists: Do you have a few monologues ready?
You: Would you like classical or contemporary?
Thriving Artists: Great. Can you belt to a high F?
You: Every day of the week!
Thriving Artists: Even better! Now, how many instruments do you play?
You: Well, I played the clarinet in high school. Does that count?
Thriving Artists: Ok, good to know. Now, can you stand on your head?
You: Huh?!
Thriving Artists: Can you juggle?
You: I'm sorry, can you repeat the question please?
Thriving Artists: Hey, this is the world we live in, folks!

Christine: Nowadays, it is not enough just to be able to sing, dance, and act. You also have to be highly proficient at an instrument (sometimes more than one). You not only have to sound beautiful as a soprano, but casting directors also want you to be able to belt out "Defying Gravity" just like Idina Menzel. Doing cartwheels and round-offs doesn't cut it anymore. Choreographers want to see handsprings and standing back tucks. I wish I were kidding.

In the golden years of Broadway there were separate singing and dancing choruses, and never-the-two-shall-meet. When *Oklahoma!* premiered at the St. James Theatre back on March 31, 1943, the singers alone crooned "Many a New Day" while the dancers separately performed all the choreography. Gone are those days of Broadway. You don't just have to be a triple threat now; you have to be more of a quadruple or quintuple threat.

As for on-camera work, the same rules apply. No longer can you simply have the ability to "play" a cop. Casting directors and producers want you to actually *be* a cop. We can't tell you how many casting breakdowns come out that say "Real professional golfers/rock climbers/construction workers/tri-athletes wanted." You name it, they are asking for the *real thing*.

A lot of young performers ask our advice for what can help them in their careers and we never hesitate to say, "Take a class, any class." Singing, acting, dancing, instrumental, acrobatics, dialect, improv are all viable and necessary. You can never start too soon and you can never have too many skills. The caveat in that is to also remember not to spread yourself too thin. Continue to hone your primary craft to a razor-sharp edge. Yes do as much as you can, but what you do, do it well.

*Christine: I have always felt that dance classes kept me working consistently. I started dancing when I was seven years old and never stopped. Tap, jazz, ballet, modern, whatever I could sign up for, I took. Also, take advantage of your parents' generosity and go to classes while they are still (hopefully) paying for them. If you do go to college, take as many extra classes as you can fit into your schedule (without killing yourself). If you are out of school and already on your own, you may find it hard to fit classes into your auditioning and job schedule, but classes are **a must** to stay viable. Saturate your body and saturate your mind. Go to the ballet. Take hip-hop. Even try checking out "Dancing with the Stars." It couldn't hurt, right? It is never too early or too late to start. "Get out those tap shoes, Francis!"*

Don't scoff at those accordion or banjo lessons. When *Cabaret* was revived on Broadway in 1998, you might have scored a job with that skill. Always remember that any skill that has to do with music, dance, or gymnastics can always help you. You want to have several tricks up your sleeve, especially when you are first starting out. You may not be the most talented singer/dancer/actor in the world, but when a show calls for breathing fire, and you can breathe fire, you just might find yourself on Broadway. Conversely, you may opt to remove gymnastics from your list of skills eventually because your body may not want to do those front walkovers anymore. However, that skill might have landed you a bunch of jobs in the past, and work begets work, right? Right. Early on, try to keep all your options open and to not limit yourself too much. Later, when your career (and body) are changing (or possibly hurting!), you can be a bit more selective about the skills that you promote. Remember, whatever you have listed on your resume, you have to be able to do eight times a week and/or believably on camera!

For quick reference, here's a short list of popular shows and the skills you are likely to need to be in them:

<u>Roller Skating</u>
And the World Goes 'Round
Starlight Express
Xanadu

<u>Stunts/Acrobatics/Cheerleading/Jump Rope</u>
Billy Elliot
Bring It On
Tarzan
Wicked
Newsies
Memphis
The Lion King
Legally Blonde

<u>Rope and Lasso Tricks</u>
Will Rogers Follies
Oklahoma

<u>Puppetry</u>
Avenue Q

<u>Instrumental Skills</u>
Million Dollar Quartet (piano, guitar)
American Idiot (guitar)
Company & Sweeney Todd (John Doyle's version) every instrument possible
Once (guitar)

<u>Equestrian Skill</u>
War Horse
Equus

<u>Voice Acting</u>
Talk Radio

As you can see from this very short list, there is no such thing as a useless skill. All those lessons over all those years just might pay off! Mom and Dad won't be so upset about shelling out all that money when they are attending the opening night of your hit show or watching you on a hit TV series every week!

To those of you who have been in the business for a while, we want you to move out of your comfort zone and think outside the box. Test yourself. If you have been to commercial auditions lately, you know that improv is constantly being asked for. So check out an improv class if you haven't yet. Try flamenco or salsa dancing. Learn to play an instrument - who knows where it might take you? Build up your special skills and keep training. Let us say that again: *Keep training*!

Christine: Joe and I both always audition better when we are in class. My callback and booking ratio is considerably higher when I am actively studying. It could be an intensive six or eight-week scene study or audition class, or it could be an ongoing class that you take each week. Whenever you are stretching yourself and getting consistency in your training it will make your work better top to bottom, and auditioning will be that much easier for you.

The next part of this Talent, Skill, and Practical Knowledge section, is knowing yourself. It is where and how you fit into the business, commonly referred to as your "type." There are people with massive amounts of "raw talent" with no idea how to focus it and make that talent pay off. To put it simply, if you do not know your type you may have a very hard time getting work. For example, a man who has an athletic build and is shorter than 5'8" is likely going to be looked at as a tumbler/dancer and be expected to have those abilities.

Joe: I've been asked countless times in auditions if I tumble. The question comes up based upon how I look and my height. I knew my type back in college and what I would be expected to do once I was in the professional environment. So all through school I took every dance class I possibly could and got into the gymnastics studio as well. I made those choices because I knew that dancing and gymnastics would enable me to book more work. In fact, I got my Equity card from Westchester Broadway Theatre's production of CATS *because of the aforementioned skills. Knowledge about yourself is essential. You have to become totally objective about how you look, how you sound, how you dance…all of it. Think of yourself like a product in a marketplace, and see where the <u>demand</u> is. Then develop your skills and abilities to meet that demand.*

Are there shows currently on Broadway that need your talents? If not, what skills do you need to develop in order to be marketable? Look at the shows out there right now. Which ones are you right for? What are their <u>demands</u>? Can you <u>supply</u> them with what they need? If you don't know what type you are, ask your teachers or friends how they see you and what parts they can envision you playing. Now ask yourself if you agree with their opinions. If you do agree then check your skill set and make sure you are up to par on everything you need to be marketable. When your skill, talent, and type are all in line, and you have the *desire* to be that type, we call this being congruent. And when you *are* congruent and all of your talents, skills, type, and desires are in line with each other, then magical things can happen very quickly!

Of course, on the flip side, what if you do not agree with others' opinion of your type? What now? You have two choices: 1.) You can change your professional perception of yourself to meet what others see, or 2.) You can fight like hell to convince everyone you are something completely different from what your initial aesthetic type may indicate. Whichever path you choose the important thing is to be 100 percent committed to developing and marketing that product - You. There is no black or white answer to the question of type. Some actors go their entire career without ever dialing into that pocket where everything clicks. Chances are that whatever you feel in your gut about yourself is most likely going to be the right thing. It's also been said that the thing you dislike the most about yourself will probably be the thing that makes you the most money! The rub of the whole situation is that your type will change as you age. So the fun never ends, folks!

Of course, for every rule there is an exception. Obviously, it will serve you well to know what your conventional type is, because when you are in the audition room, you want to make sure that your physical look is in line with what the casting people are looking for. You need to know the character breakdown, because that is what guides the audition and casting decisions (product → marketplace). Your callback and booking ratio will go through the roof once you are congruent. Or, and this is the beautiful and maddening part of this business, your callback and booking ratio will go through the roof because you are so confidently playing *against* your type, and landing the work because of it. Either way, you have to know exactly what your type is before you can make any informed choice to go with it or against it.

2. Book Knowledge
This is a simple step in getting yourself in or keeping yourself in the game from an information standpoint. Book knowledge is nothing more than what it implies: knowing your craft from a historical perspective, and being up to date on what is happening now. Simply put, you need to know which projects are currently being cast and which casting offices are involved. What books are being optioned? What films are in development? What Broadway shows are in the pipeline and who are the people directing and choreographing them? What are the top five casting agencies in New York or LA (or wherever you are)? What projects are those offices currently casting for, and should you be pursuing that work? Check out Playbill.com, IMDBPro.com, The Ross Reports, etc. to seek out this information.

Anytime you are going in for an audition look to see who's who before you get there. If you are at an Equity audition (one run by Actors' Equity Association) you will always be able to see a written list of who's in the room and what their role is with the project. If you don't know who they are, research them on Google or IBDB.com (Internet Broadway Database) and keep track of this information. Then, when you have a chance meeting in the elevator, you'll know whom you are talking to. It happens all the time on the way to an audition, and if they like you as a human being, they just might take a second look and give you a callback. Always keep a finger on what is going on in your business, because it is good business to do so!

Note: A great way to keep track of who's who is with a journal/spreadsheet either on your computer or hand written. A book we love is The Organized Actor *by Leslie Becker; it has a brilliant tracking system for this type of information. It's the number-one organizational tool for actors and it's easy to carry with you. Check it out!*

3. Professional Knowledge

Professional knowledge is commonly referred to as "experience": the knowledge you gain through working in your field. You can be the most well-trained person in the world who is able to do back flips in roller skates whilst playing the tuba and naming every single person who has ever worked on a Broadway show since the dawn of time. Understand that none of that does you one bit of good, if you don't act and present yourself like a professional!

But what exactly does "act and present yourself like a professional" mean?

Simple. It means be prepared, do brilliant work, and then go home. It means don't be a nonstop-shop-talking-ass-kissing-ambition-oozing-jerk. It means being your own person, the kind that other people are going to want to hire and work with. All the talent and know-how in the world will never eclipse the fact that if everyone knows you are a nightmare to work with, you are done. You might land a job here and there, but you also may find yourself in the unemployment line rather than in the chorus line more often than you anticipated.

It also means that you need to know how to behave and work in a professional environment. You have to be aware of divisions of labor and protocol, meaning you should know and respect the duties and boundaries of other people in the theatre, on set, etc. Some of this you may already know but it's always good to touch on the basics. Let's look at some examples in the theatrical workplace:

Example #1. Never walk across the stage at intermission without first asking permission from the technical director or a stage manager. A professional actor understands that the deck officially belongs to the TD or SM as they are changing out set pieces and getting ready for Act II. The stage can be a very hazardous environment and actors get hurt all the time for being careless, disrespectful, or uneducated about protocol.

Example #2. This is a big one. When a director, dance captain or stage manager is giving you a note, just shut up and take the note! There is no need to defend, justify, or make any excuse at all. It is not personal! It is business, and you are part of creating a product. They are giving you a note to make the show better and it doesn't matter whether or you agree with it or not. It also doesn't matter if you *like* the person giving you the correction. Your job as a performer is to listen, understand, and say thank you. Of course, ask questions if you need to, but resist the urge to talk about it at length, because it does you no good. The note will be the same after you have talked it into the ground as it was before you got it.

Joe: I have been on both sides of that fence in both giving notes as a dance captain and taking notes as a performer. I know from giving notes how easy it is when someone simply listens and says thank you, and how difficult it can be when someone has to talk to me for five minutes about why their way of doing something is justified. Trust me, when getting a note (and I have received many) I fully understand the deep desire to explain why I was doing something the way I was doing it. (For those of you out there who have given me notes that I talked about too much, I do apologize! J) The fact of the matter is you need to take the note and do as it says. In other words, just fix it! A true professional will accept the note, smile, nod, and say thank you! As you are working to build a reputation of being a professional, acceptance of constructive criticism is part of the deal. Your career and your bank account will thank you for it.

Example #3. At some point in your career you are bound to work with a very well known celebrity. Treat them like a human being.

Christine: I was in my mid-20's when I joined the touring cast of The Best Little Whorehouse in Texas, *starring Ann-Margret. I had never really come in contact with a big star and certainly hadn't worked intimately with one. I wasn't quite sure how to act. I was a replacement in the company so everyone already knew each other. We all know how important first impressions are! Do I just walk up and introduce myself? Do I hang back and wait to be introduced? I went for the latter. I hung back, watched everyone else as they interacted with her, and waited to meet this star that I admired. Turned out that I made the right decision - we are still in contact to this day!*

Some other professional courtesies to remember in the actor's world:

1. **Be nice to every single person in an audition setting - especially the accompanist and the monitor.**
    The accompanist might be the musical director and the monitor might be the director's personal assistant. In many cases, the personal assistant is the eyes and ears of the musical director, the director, or the producers, and how you treat people will be duly noted.

2. **Do not give notes to another actor...ever!**
    It should go without saying, but *never give a fellow actor a note.* If you are having an issue with another actor in your show, always go to the dance captain and/or production stage manager for choreography or scene staging respectively. Giving notes to other actors is the fastest way to create tension and animosity between you and the rest of the cast.

3. **Be nice to swings and understudies when they go on!**
    They are doing the best they can and need your support. Nothing undermines a swing/understudy's confidence more than rolling your eyes at them or being unwilling to adjust for their style of performance. Yes, it is their job to perform the same role as the full-time cast member, but we are all different human beings so wiggle room is very much appreciated. Can you tell we've both been swings?

4. **When on tour do your very best not to call out of the second show on a load-out day (usually a Sunday).**
    Load out for the crew of any tour is a very long night and timed within an inch of its life. If you call out for the second show on a Sunday before travel, it creates a lot more work for every department to get your costumes/mics/wigs out, get the swing's costumes/mics/wigs in, and then get everything packed up and ready for the move. So if you are in for a penny, be in for a pound unless you are severely injured or deathly ill! Your crew will thank you for it.

5. **While at the touring theater house, or on location with a film (or ever for that matter) do not talk poorly about the city you are in.** **
The entire local crew calls that city home. It is very rude and it reflects poorly on the whole company.

Wow, that was a ton of information! Lets take a quick look back at what we covered in this first chapter.

- First, *decide* that you are indeed a Thriving Artist. Think like one and act like one and your life will align accordingly...not the other way around. Control your inner world and you can create anything in your outer world. Mind over matter.

- Who you are is as important as what you do and the skills you possess.

- Knowledge of yourself, your talent, your skills, and your industry are critical to building a thriving career.

Chapter 3 - Focus On: Goals

Getting specific about what you want, when, and how to make it happen

> "If you don't know where you are going, you'll end up someplace else."
> — *Yogi Berra*

We cannot stress enough the importance of goals. Of course you want to work as an artist. Who doesn't? Your ultimate goal may be Broadway, a regular on a sitcom, penning the next Pulitzer, or having your work on display at the J. Paul Getty Center. Whatever your goal may be, we truly believe you can get there.

But you can't get anywhere if you don't know where you are going! So you have to be specific - *extremely* specific about what you want and when you want it. You should be able to describe your goal in every sensory detail, so that it is a living, breathing thing for you. The more emotionally charged your goal is, the faster it will be drawn to you. The "charge" electrifies your emotions, so that they act like a magnet allowing your goal to gravitate toward you at lightening speed.

However, a goal and some good feelings aren't enough. We need *action*!

We like the saying, "A goal without a plan is just a wish." Once the goal is in mind you align all your thoughts, feelings, and actions with it. You are in a state of congruence with your goal and everything it takes to achieve it, and the result is you achieving your goal as if by magic. But it happened because you *made* it happen! You had a well-thought-out goal, the right attitude, and took focused and inspired action.

Take a look at your goal(s), and then ask, "Who else has achieved something similar to what I want to achieve?" Look at who they are and what they did to make it happen. Finally, ask yourself, "Who do I need to *be*, and what do I need to *do* so that this can happen as quickly as possible?" It all builds on your thoughts, feelings, actions, knowledge bases, and belief that you *can* achieve what you want in the first place! See how this all works?

*Joe: I remember from the time I was in high school, Broadway was **it**. Period. I graduated high school and moved on to Penn State to study in their Musical Theatre Program. I wasn't at all concerned with getting good grades or passing the classes because I was constantly asking myself, "Where do I need to be when I get out of here? What do I need to do in order to be marketable?" I had a singular focus, because I knew exactly what my goal was. I realized that if I was only working to get an A or to please the teacher, that would not matter when I got "out there." I knew that out there, I would have to be a cut above everybody else in order to be competitive as a theatrical professional. I needed to be better, and that also meant holding myself to a professional standard, not a collegiate one. I kept my focus and made it to Broadway in just a few short years after graduating college. I have always seen show business as just that: a business. Many artists, unfortunately, see show business as a crapshoot, and become speculative about their goals. They may think about their goals with the words "I hope this will happen" or "I sure am trying." Successful artists think about their goals with the words, "This is <u>going to happen</u>" or better yet, "This is already happening." The difference between these thoughts is game changing. If you are merely going through your days hoping to make your goals a reality, you may wake up several years down the road and be very under-whelmed with what you have (or haven't) achieved. By actively envisioning and working toward your goals, rather than hoping, you may be completely elated with what you <u>have</u> achieved.*

Where do you want to be in one, three, or five years? It's always to your advantage to have a long-term outlook. With that in mind, you also need to know where you want to be in one, three, or five months!

As time goes on, evaluate your actions and enhance them as needed so your goal is realistic and attainable by your target date. Every goal needs a target date for completion, but know that it's no big deal if the date for accomplishing your goal changes. The important thing is that you have a specific target to aim at. Life happens and there is no need to stress over missing a self-imposed benchmark. Just adjust your target date to reflect what is actually happening so you stay congruent with your thoughts, feelings, and actions. Build on your successes and keep at it until it's done! (We changed the date of finishing this book at least nine or ten times!)

Christine: *"I want to be on Broadway by the time I'm thirty!" How many of us have said this or something similar? How many of us got there? Who didn't yet? Notice the "yet!" Excellent! So, if you're like me, on your thirtieth birthday you may have to adjust and push it back a little bit, and that is ok. You have to be flexible and maybe re-evaluate. Just keep at it…I am!*

A great example of having a focused goal becoming a reality is the case of Cameron Mackintosh, who was Christine's producer for *My Fair Lady*. Mackintosh produced his first show at eight years old. *Eight years old!* He knew exactly what he wanted to do and made it happen without an ounce of hesitation. Brilliant!

To know exactly what you want to do at such a young age is a blessing, because it creates clarity, and clarity is the gateway to rapid goal achievement. We are not suggesting that if you do not have a clear goal at eight years of age, you should be worried. We are saying that your goal(s) should always be clear and congruent with your thoughts, feelings, and actions. Design a goal and give that goal a target date for completion. You have to know where the bull's-eye is so you know where to aim. If you miss it, no sweat, and once again you can evaluate and adjust. The important thing is to stay focused on that bull's-eye and keep aiming your thoughts, feelings, and actions at the center.

The Details
Let's get specific about your goals.

This first thing to do is get a notebook or five separate pieces of paper. We are going to separate your goals into different categories so that we can analyze them more easily.

This part should be fun! Take your time and do it in a quiet place with no distractions. Challenge yourself to write down as many goals as you can/want. Dig deep, and don't hold back! Write some goals that are immediately within your reach and also write some that will stretch you way beyond your current limits. There is no right or wrong here, and no list can be too long or too short. Your spiritual goals may take up only half of a page but your career goals could be front and back. Just go with it.

Here are your topics followed by some examples in each to get your brains popping: Put each topic on a separate sheet of paper.

1. Career/Business Goals

2. Family Goals

3. Personal Goals

4. Spiritual Goals

5. Financial/Material Goals

Career / Business Goals examples:
Get nominated for a Tony Award
Have a recurring role on a TV show
Make a CD of my music
Perform at the Public Theatre
Have my music played on the radio
Get on American Idol and win
Have my new musical picked for the NYMF festival
Have a gallery showing of my artwork

Family Goals examples:
Support my family in every way possible
Have two wonderful children
Give my family my time and energy
Continually learn how to be a good parent
Adopt a child
Adopt a pet

Personal Goals examples:
Go to at least one concert a year
Take a hot air balloon ride
Hike the Grand Canyon
Attend the Super Bowl/Indy 500/World Series
Stay in great shape and learn more about nutrition
Use a new recipe every week/month
Travel the seven continents
Build homes for Habitat for Humanity

Spiritual Goals examples:

Become a leader in my church/synagogue/place of worship

Use my musical talents to improve the services at my place of worship

Volunteer my time, especially during the holidays, to those in need

Be able to tithe 10 percent of my income to help in any way it can

Financial / Material Goals examples:

Open a Roth IRA

Save a certain amount every month/year

Learn more about mutual/money market funds

Invest in the stock market

Own property

Always pay off credit card every month

Start college fund for children

Take vacation of choice at least once a year

Have a beach/vacation home

Be able to retire early and comfortably

> ## "Most people overestimate what they can do in a year, but underestimate what they can do in ten"
> ### *- Anthony Robbins*

Often, when people make their New Year's resolutions, those good intentions end up being way more than they can do in one calendar year and they set themselves up for a fall. Do some prioritizing, spread your goals out, and get realistic. It *can* all be yours, just not all at once!

Set yourself up for success. Choose one or two things from each category that are intensely important to you and focus on them. You may also want to have a few other goals that you can get started on right away in case you get something big done sooner than you thought. Amazing things happen when you create laser focus and take action! You may find yourself checking things off way ahead of time.

And yes, have at least one real juicy, awe-inspiring, *unreasonable* goal! Why not? Play big! Create a goal that makes you pee yourself just a little bit! Something that makes you go, "Whoa, did I just say that?" Try something like, "I am standing opposite _____ in a year doing a scene in a feature film." And name someone like Meryl Streep, or someone who is seemingly so far out of your network that you don't know how you are going to get there. Still, you speak it, believe it, take action on it, and the Universe lines up to help you make it happen. Not to get too crunchy-granola-metaphysical, but, the law of attraction works, y'all!

What next?

The next step is to prioritize your goals. What are your most important projects right now? Be smart about this. If one of your career goals is to star in a Broadway show and you have just graduated college, then your immediate priorities may be working on a national tour, regional theatre, workshops of new shows, or Off-Broadway. Of course, you might just land your starring role on Broadway next week; statistics prove otherwise. Someone with little experience getting that opportunity is rare, but yes it does happen. Someone with leads at Goodspeed Opera House, The Guthrie, Mark Taper Forum, a major national tour, and some TV credits etc. is much more likely to get that opportunity. So while you will hold that huge goal in your mind and heart, you may need to work at it incrementally. Adding in some more goals like doing regional work, playing a lead in a national tour, booking a co-star spot on a hit TV show, etc. may be necessary before the big goal manifests itself.

Prioritize your goals into three time frames: Short-term, mid-term, and long-term. The times we allot below for each type of goal are always subject to change. What is short-term for one person may be long-term for another. Always plan in time frames that are conceivable to you.

Short-term goals – Achieved between now and eighteen months
Mid-term goals – Achieved eighteen months to three years
Long-term goals – Achieved three years and beyond

Write down next to each goal whether it is short-term, mid-term, or long-term. Or you can highlight your goals in different colors...whatever works for you.

Once you have done that, we are going to focus mainly on defining and crystallizing your short-term goals. These short-term goals may fall in line with a longer-term goal, but for now just focus on what is attainable in the next eighteen months.

For example: Under your financial goals, perhaps you wrote that you wanted to own a property. Where is the property? Is it a house or condo? How many bedrooms? What is the price? What are the monthly mortgage and tax payments that are doable for you? Does it have a stainless steel kitchen? A fireplace?

Perhaps you wrote down a career goal to make a CD of your own music. How many songs? What style do you want to play in? How many instruments do you need/want in the band? Who would you like to collaborate with? Will you record a duet with someone you know and admire?

This exercise will eliminate any guesswork, so you then know *exactly* what you are working toward. The more specific you are, the better.

QUICK CONTEXT SHIFT

So many of us *want* things, and that's great, but simply wanting them isn't enough to get off your backside to make them a reality. Saying, "I want" is a statement that spawns no creative thought whatsoever. It is fine to want things, but we need to make a shift in our thinking. Take the list of things you want and then ask yourself, *"How can I make that happen?"* Immediately your brain goes into problem-solving mode. You can't stop it. Ask a question long enough and you *will* come up with an answer. It may not be the answer you imagined it would be, but you'll have a path nonetheless. If you really want to play big, ask yourself really big questions! For example, if getting to Broadway is your goal there are several ways of asking.

1. How can I get to Broadway?
2. How can I get to Broadway as fast as possible?
3. How can I get to Broadway in a leading/supporting role in three years?

Are you getting the idea? The quality of your results can be predicted by the quality of your question. So ask a good one and then let your brain work on the solution!

> "Always the beautiful answer who asks a more beautiful question."
> **- e. e. cummings**

THE "HOW" OF ACHIEVING YOUR GOALS

After you have a crystal-clear vision of your goal(s) and an end date, you have to work backwards for a moment. Start at the target achievement date and break down what you need to do on a month-to-month basis to realize that goal. Once you have the monthly goal, break it into four weekly goals. Go one last step and determine what you need to do on a daily basis by breaking the weekly goal into as many days per week as you can realistically dedicate your time. Now you have a clear road map of exactly what you need to do to make your goal happen by your target date.

The next step is to eat, sleep, and breathe your goal(s). Talk about them as if you are already in possession of them. Create a goal affirmation sheet and/or a vision board.

Goal Affirmation Sheet: a list of your goals or long-form paragraph that you write out and look at every day, several times a day. This keeps your goals in the center of your mind and magnetizes you. We will break this down even further a bit later in this chapter.

Vision Board: a visual representation (pictures/drawings/cutouts) of your realized goals. You can put whatever you want up there that crystallizes what your goals look like. Cut out pictures of houses, cars, awards, vacation spots…whatever gives you chills and gets your blood pumping, put it up there. The more specific it is, the better. Look at it every morning when you get up and every night before you go to sleep. Focus on it. Give it energy and again, you will magnetize yourself to those things.

THRIVING POINT

When talking about your goals avoid using words like "hope" or "try." Speak about everything as if it is a given or in the process of happening. Keep your thoughts and words in the positive. As you open yourself up to this way of thinking and speaking, the Universe will reward you. You will suddenly come upon other artists who are writing/producing their own CDs and can offer you studio space for a fraction of the price. Or they know the greatest sound mixer on the planet. Those "coincidences" will start to add up and move you toward your finish line!

As you begin to achieve your short-term goals, it's time to move on and look at your mid-term goals. Your mid-term goals have now become your new short-term goals. Now that those long-term goals aren't so far off in the distance, they seem a bit more attainable.

We want you to know what you have to do every day, every week, and every month to achieve your dreams. How much money will it take? How much time? If you want a master's from Yale in acting then it's probably a minimum of four years: one to audition and three to go through the program. It may also cost a pretty penny. You could possibly get a lot of money in scholarship or teaching stipends but you can't always count on that so you have to be realistic about how you are going to pay for it.

So let's look at those short-term goals again. We can also add in some of those mid-term goals, especially the ones that go hand in hand with the short-term goals. Let's take five short-term and three mid-term goals (for our example below we will only look at one of each). We all only have twenty-four hours in a day (eighteen if we only sleep for six of them). Here is the blueprint for goal achievement:

First short-term goal and today's date: _____

     Books and/or people that will help me achieve this goal:

     Classes, seminars, and trainings I must attend to achieve this goal:

     How much $$ each month:

     How much $$ total necessary:

     How much time each week:

     How much total time needed:

     Date of achievement:

Does this help put things a little more into perspective? Let's do one or two of the goals together.

First short-term goal and today's date: Play a lead at Papermill Playhouse; April 24, 20___

Books and/or people that will help me achieve this goal: read biographies on other successful actors, "how-to" books

Classes, seminars, and trainings I must attend to achieve this goal: Voice lessons (need new teacher), musical theatre class

How much $$ each month: $167.00 a month

How much $$ total necessary: $1500.00 in classes and lessons

How much time each week: one-hour lesson every other week, three-hour musical theatre class every week, work at home: total eight hours/week

How much total time needed: six months

Date of Achievement: October 24, 20____

Mid-term goal and today's date: Own an apartment: June 6, 20____

Books and/or people that will help me achieve this goal: *Rich Dad, Poor Dad* by Robert Kiyosaki, Suze Orman's books on money management

Classes, seminars, and trainings I must attend to achieve this goal: real estate class, mortgage class

How much $$ total necessary: I want to buy a one-bedroom for $450,000. I need a minimum $45,000 down payment and $10,000 in closing costs (say $60,000 total to be safe)

How much total time needed: I already have $40,000 saved, so saving $500.00 a month means I would have an extra $21,000 in three and a half years

How much $$ each month: $500.00

How much time to devote each week: Need to work a 40-hour week making $30/hour

Date of Achievement: December 6, 20____

Let's go back to breaking down your goals. Say you have five short-term goals and three mid-term goals in your columns. You need to add up the monthly income columns and how much time is needed to earn that amount. If the time needed is more than 126 hours, you must redefine your goals or move the target date. We are basing this on having eighteen hours a day, seven days a week. If you have a 30-to 40-hour-per-week job, which most of us do, then you probably only have 86 to 96 hours a week; and this does not factor in errands, seeing shows, movies, and hanging out with friends. Remember to be realistic, so after looking at the actual time you will have, you might need to readjust your target date.

The other column that may need some attention is the money column. How much monthly income will it take to fund the achievement of these goals? If it's a number that you cannot meet with your current income then you need to create more or adjust your date to match what you are currently doing. There is no shame in moving the date because of money! Your journey is your journey and you have bills and rent to pay. We get it - this is life. *Set yourself up for success by creating goals you can realistically attain.* Small successes over time will add up to the big one you had your eye on from the get-go.

Depending on how your brain works, "big picture" thinking may not be your strong suit. You may want to do three short-term goals and one mid-term goal that are in line with a long-term goal. The point is that you break any goal into little pieces and use a system to achieve it based on whatever you can *realistically* implement and stick to over time. Whatever works for you, do it and stick with it. Consistency is very important in your goal achievement. We all know people who joined the gym in January, went for a month, and then never went again. Remaining focused, doing little things every day, every week, and every month gets things done. Stay the course!

THE PATH AND THE OBSTACLES

The next step is figuring out what you will do, give up, or overcome to attain these goals? Are you one of those people who *must* have the latest fashions and the newest gadgets? Do you hate to cook, so you find yourself eating out more often? These are the kinds of questions to ask yourself, because until you reach your goals, some habits may have to change for a while. The important point here is to make conscious and informed choices about your actions and how they affect achievement of your goals, especially when you find out how much your goals are going to cost. To seriously take action and make your goals a reality, the purse strings might have to tighten, and/or you have to become hyper-aware of every penny coming in and going out. If you are a fashion junkie and you spend a lot of money on clothing, start getting creative with your wardrobe and recycle old clothes. Have a clothing swap with your friends and remain the trendy fashion queen without spending a dime. You may have never thought about your life in these terms, or perhaps you had not seen how your goals were actually possible. Open yourself up to new ways of thinking and you may find a way to make it happen. Everything is possible.

Consider this:

What if you lived in suburbia and the only way to get to your job was to drive? The options to take a subway, hop on the bus, or grab a cab are unavailable. Then one day your trusty chariot breaks down. It is going to cost $600 in repairs. Are you going to find a way to get that $600? Of course you are! So why don't we do the same thing when it comes to our life's dreams and goals?

Take a moment to really think about this…is there anything you have to overcome? Do you have a fear of the unknown? Do friends and family not support you? Are the people at your job negative and always bringing you down? Might you have a touch of laziness? Are you watching too much TV? Are you unable to follow through and finish what you start?

If you answered, "yes" to one or more of these questions, then it is important to realize that those issues must be dealt with if you are going to reach your goals. Do you think that Gene Kelly watched a ton of TV and had half-finished projects lying around? We doubt that Alfred Hitchcock was lazy. We have a feeling that they were up before anyone else and stayed on set after everyone else had gone home.

So ask yourself, what obstacles will you overcome to achieve your goals?

Time management?

Money issues?

Lifestyle/non-supportive environment?

Sacrifices?

From the short list above, can you identify areas for self-improvement?

After these realizations, you may have to (once again) go back and fine-tune your target dates for reaching your goals. You may be unyielding in your brunch time on Sundays with your girlfriends. That is fine. "All work and no play" can wear you out and balance is important. Christine lives by the motto: "Work Hard, Play Hard." You may have religious duties that consume either your Saturday or Sunday. No problem.

Whatever your challenges are, just be honest about them. We hope that through some of these exercises you have gotten a clearer picture of just how much time, money, etc. you need to devote to your goals. Take a truthful look at your life and how it will help or hinder your achievement, and then adjust accordingly. Clarity is power.

TOOLS TO HELP YOU ALONG THE WAY

To achieve any goal, no matter how far away it is, a Goal Affirmation Sheet is a tool that can help you. If you don't write down your goals and/or tell them to someone, they're just a wish. When you actually put weight to them, pen to paper, you have something tangible for guidance. Writing down goals and sharing them also puts you on the hook to make them happen. Ask the people who love you and want to see you succeed to hold you accountable.

Your Goal Affirmation Sheet can be in paragraph form, or you may choose to just have a list of bullet points. Maybe you just want to cut out pictures of what you want and put them on your wall in the form of a Vision Board. Whatever energizes you to take action is what you should do. There is no "right" answer here. However you represent your goals, they take the best root when you refer to them several times a day. Place them in prominent places around your apartment/house and put a copy in your wallet as well. If you *really* want to put yourself on the hook, tape a list of your goals to the front of the TV and see if your viewing hours decrease!

IMPORTANT: When creating your Goal Affirmation Sheet in paragraph form, write it as a reflection from a future date and include at least one specific from the immediate past tense. So you'll start by saying,

"It is July 4, 20___, and all of these fireworks are for me and what I've accomplished! Since February 4 of this year (the date you are actually writing your sheet) I have been an example of efficiency as I easily did the work of three people. I am jumping out of my skin because my new musical is being presented this year at the New York Musical Theater Festival, and there is interest in it going all the way to Broadway! I am overflowing with dynamic energy, gratitude, and love."

   - It is important to put positive emotions into your statement. As noted before, the more emotion you have about something, the faster it will come to you. Imagine what it will feel like when you have reached your goal. Then include that in your Goal Affirmation Sheet.

After listing the things you have accomplished and how you feel about them, continue to talk about your actions as if they have already happened!

For example, "... I happily turned off the television and worked on my show for an extra hour every single day and it did wonders for my productivity. My writing team all kept up on their assignments and the whole creative process was a joy..."

- You are actively programming your brain to automatically do what you need to do and overcome any obstacle you might have identified earlier.

You can continue on in this manner for as many goals as you have set for that given date. When ending your Goal Affirmation Sheet, be sure to add a compelling future focus that carries you forward, as you continue your habit of successful behavior for future achievements.

For example, "Over the past six months, I have developed habits and new ways of being that I have learned all successful people share. I am on time, impeccable with my word, and enthusiastic about other people's success. As I move forward, I am excited to know that I can manage my time to the minute and my money to the penny. I can do *anything* when I put my mind to it."

- Ending with a declarative statement as to what you are capable of and what you have mastered will further imprint it on your subconscious, making it part of your natural way of being.

Phrases like "I want/will/wish/hope/try...etc" are not useful or powerful because they leave room for something not to happen - in short, they make it OK for you to fail. Statements like "I am" and "I have" are more beneficial and program your brain in a powerful and positive way. Here is an example of a complete Goal Affirmation Sheet in paragraph from:

"It is June 9, 20___, and I am over the moon to have just finished playing my first leading role at Goodspeed Opera House! I received rave reviews, and have three auditions lined up with new agents who are excited about my work. I am also auditioning at the very top of my game and it is a joy to walk into the room, because I know I am fully prepared. Since April 2 of this year I have been taking one theater class and one voice lesson every week and it has paid off tenfold. I've been getting a callback at 85 percent of my auditions! I have had numerous callbacks for Broadway shows and all the major casting directors (Rubin, Binder, Telsey, Carnahan, etc.) know who I am. I easily get in the room for any audition they are

holding. I feel at home in my own skin. I am a leading lady and everyone is seeing me that way. I have loved saving a minimum of $100 a week to purchase my new apartment and am also earning $150/month in interest with Capital One 360. I am through reading Rich Dad, Poor Dad *and will be taking my first mortgage seminar July 15. Through all of the activity, I had time to reach my goal weight, too! I have been working out four days per week and have lost two inches off my waist! I am a powerhouse of a human being and I love the world I am living in. I bring joy to everyone I encounter and, in so doing, bring joy to every corner of the earth. This is who I am, and this is who I create myself to be every day. The future is mine for the taking."* Signed, Christine Negherbon

Now, say that June 9 has come and gone and you have not lost the two inches nor finished reading *Rich Dad, Poor Dad*. Fine. Adjust and keep going.

Creating a crystal-clear affirmation sheet will give you a roadmap to achieving your goals. No more flying by the seat of your pants and *hoping* you save enough money to buy that apartment. No more looking back at the previous year wondering what you did or didn't accomplish.

Life doesn't "just happen." Life is what *you create*. So start *consciously* creating! Make it beautiful. Make it inspiring. Make it yours!

Strategies for Time Management
<u>Come up with a weekly plan</u> – If your workweek starts on Monday, then you will devise your weekly plan Sunday night. If your week starts on Sunday, you will be planning on Saturday. You *must* decide what specific goals you are going to accomplish that week, because if you don't, it will be Friday and you might wonder where the week went. You may also find that you got pushed into other people's schedules because you didn't have your own. Plan your week according to what *you* need to accomplish and to the very best of your ability stick with your plan!

<u>Make a to-do list each night</u> – This is something that has really proven helpful for us. Every night before we go to bed, we write out all the things we will get done the next day. If you see your daily tasks in writing, then you are more likely to feel the need to get them done. You will also feel a sense of accomplishment at the end of every day when you cross them all off!

Here is an example of a to-do list. Specificity works wonders! Instead of a general item like "work out," try "run five miles and stretch." There is no need to micro manage here, but getting more focused will make your time and effort more productive.

Get up at 8:30 a.m.
Make a healthy breakfast: egg whites w/ spinach
Work on screenplay for one hour (*Be specific:* i.e., write two scenes for X character)
Go to the gym (take cardio aerobics class)
Make five phone calls to my Pilates clients
Pay credit card and cell phone bills online
Clean bathroom
Go to the post office – mail thank-you cards
Sing for a half an hour (be specific about what songs and/or exercises)

By utilizing a more focused daily goals sheet you set yourself up for much more efficient and effective actions throughout the day. We know firsthand the power of lists like these especially now that we have a child!

Delegate – This has been a difficult lesson for us to learn, because both of us always think (for better or worse) that we can do everything more effectively than anyone else. You might find that you get only a few things done on your list and then you are exhausted and frustrated with a to-do list that never shrinks. A wonderful way to avoid the exhaustion and the frustration of a never-shrinking to-do list is to *delegate* some of the tasks. Check out your contact list and see if you know people who might like doing some of the tasks you would rather avoid. Also examine the possibility of bartering selected tasks on your list with those on someone else's. You also want to keep your list to a realistic number of tasks because, let's face it, there are only so many hours in the day. There are no bad jobs, just the wrong person doing the wrong job…so find people who will love doing what you suck at! Everybody needs a team.

Be accountable - A really good thing to start is an accountability group. This can be with people that you know from college, work, or wherever. It's a very small group that holds you accountable to your goals. So when you say to this group, "OK, I'm going to do X, Y, and Z over the next three months" by sharing it and speaking it, it becomes real. You can't hide it anymore, because you verbalized it to others and they will hold you to it. Now you are putting yourself on the hook for real! Everyone makes excuses, but not you, if you are *serious* about being a Thriving Artist. All the excuses have to go away. Share your goals, put yourself on the playing field, and go do it!

We can say from experience that starting or joining a goal setting/accountability group is a brilliant idea, especially when you first get to the city or have been there a while and are feeling stagnant or isolated. We can all get bogged down in our family issues and everyday life and lose our focus. It is just life! So having people you trust, who are objective and maybe even a little hard on you, will be invaluable in keeping you on track. We are not saying that this is a competition with others. It *is* about personal best, and so, if one of your group booked a Broadway show or released a hit new CD, be happy for his/her achievement. The only person you are in competition with is you. Everyone's goals are going to be different and they are going to be achieved in different time frames. So tap some friends on the shoulder and set up a weekly meeting of the minds. You will be amazed at what can happen!

<u>Be disciplined and consistent</u> - This is probably the most important. If you say you are going to do something, do it. If you put something on your list for Monday and you don't get to it, then roll it over to Tuesday. If you stay strict about this you will get everything done. We have to be the drill sergeant in our own minds. No one but you will ever know if you don't paint that masterpiece (that you are fully capable of creating!).

TO WRAP UP

We cannot stress enough the importance of knowing where you are going and having a detailed plan of action to get there. Artists who have multiple streams of income, successful careers, and busy home lives probably do not turn on the TV much or obsess over the latest level of Angry Birds. Using the tools and tips outlined here will keep you on track, accountable, and motivated. Do whatever it takes to make your goals become reality! We believe in you!

Chapter 4 - Focus On: Seeing and Being Seen
The Art of Marketing and Selling

We cannot state strongly enough the importance of marketing as an artist. There are entire books written and coaches making their livelihood just on this one topic alone. Simply put, people only know about you what *you* tell them, and that process of revealing who you are is marketing. Some may call it sharing, or enrolling, or broadcasting. The point is, you're getting the word out about yourself. *How* you go about doing that, well, therein lies the art of it.

OK, so, who loves the word "selling?" Be honest. To many people, "selling," means you are trying to push someone into buying something they don't want. But here's the reality: *Everybody is selling something!* Every profession in this world comes down to selling a product or service of some kind, and that is what makes the world go around. You are a part of that world, so get used to the idea that you are selling a product too - and that product is *you*! If you aren't in love with the word "selling" then feel free to use another one. We like to say "promote" or "relay the value" of something. Here's a list of synonyms for selling. Pick one that feels right to you:

Elevate
    Advance
        Advocate
            Promote
                Hype
                    Boost
                        Endorse
                            Campaign
                                Champion

Use whatever terminology you feel comfortable with, but never forget that it is ultimately all about *selling*. We do not want you to get "weirded out" by the concept, because all Thriving Artists are very adept and comfortable with selling their product.

We touched on this a bit in our *Focus On: You* chapter, in that you have to know what your "type" is for casting purposes. The perspective you need to have is that the world of your art is like a marketplace. Thinking about yourself as a product, you must always ask yourself, "Is my product currently in demand right now?" You should be aware of what is selling on the market at any given moment. Coming to the marketplace promoting something that nobody wants is just bad business. Raise your awareness and do your research on what is out there and what the trends are.

The components that make up this Focus Area are your Brand/Content, your Marketplace, and your Platform for getting your Brand/Content out there. Let's now break down the components for selling and marketing yourself.

CONTENT
This is simple. As an artist, are you a dancer? Singer? Actor? Composer? Painter? Sculptor? Fire-eater? Another way of looking at it is just saying, "What talents do I have?" "What are my strongest products?"

MARKETPLACE
The Marketplace is essentially the "arena" where you bring your talents/products to sell. Sometimes the market doesn't necessarily want what you are selling, but you have options, 1. You can either change or update your content to meet the current market conditions, or 2. You can seek out a market where your content is wanted. Let's take a closer look at both options.

Option 1. If you are more of a traditional musical theatre singer and everything on Broadway has a pop sound, you'll have to update/change your songbook and sound if you want to be viable in that market.

Option 2. If you are that same traditional musical theatre singer who has *no interest* in learning how to change your sound, then you create your own show and find places to perform (e.g., fringe festivals, cabarets, cruise ships).

If you are determined to create a market for yourself by doing your own work/ writing your own show, you can get some serious attention if you are persistent.

Take a look at all of the web series that are being created now by actors/writers/ producers who are gaining tons of attention (and ad revenue) from putting their own work out there and carving out a niche for themselves. The market didn't exist for their content, so they created one.

THE PLATFORM

This is the place where people can see your content. It could be an art gallery, an audition room, a cabaret performance, the Internet (YouTube, your website, funny or DIE), a Broadway stage, a movie theater, or national television. Wherever it is, it is the place that allows people to have access to you and your work. The larger the platform is, the more opportunity for people to see what you do. Sometimes your content will dictate what platform you primarily use, but you can always be creative and cross-pollinate mediums to really fire on all cylinders. It all depends on how big you want to play when choosing where to exhibit your art.

YOUR BRAND

This is, essentially, what you are known for. It is a great thing, and it can be something you continually expand throughout your entire career. You hear a lot about corporations controlling or improving on their "brand image" and you should do the same - because after all, you are the CEO of You, Inc.

Joe: In my case, my "brand" has played out in working in Broadway shows and being the swing. The swing is expected to cover several roles and doing this job well is a highly valued commodity in the Broadway community. I am grateful for the ability to do it, but that was never my goal. Now that I have done two shows as a swing (Hairspray and Shrek the Musical) it could very easily become something that takes over if I'm not careful. I've heard so many swings who are upset at where they are, because they keep getting hired as swings and not as part of the nightly performing cast. But being a swing has become their brand. If you continue to take one kind of work, it is likely you will continue to get offered that same kind of work. You may have allowed yourself to be branded as something not in line with your ultimate goal. I have experienced this, and I am in the process of breaking out of it as this book is being written. Again, I am grateful in so many ways for what I have done, but the time has come to "re-brand" myself to fit my career goals. It's never to late to reinvent yourself! Just ask Betty White.

The point of saying all this is that you have to be mindful of what you allow your brand to become. The fact is that some of it you can control, and some of it you can't. Mainly we just want you to be very conscious of the process that makes it happen. The first thing you become known for can be the hardest thing to break out of, should you want to bring some new talents to the table or be seen in a different light. Your awareness of the process up front will give you a higher probability of becoming known for the things you want to be known for, rather than things that seem to "just happen" in your career.

> "A brand is a living entity - and it is enriched or
> undermined cumulatively over time, the product of a
> thousand small gestures."
> **- Michael Eisner**

Again we must mention that being a Thriving Artist is very much about awareness and bringing consciousness to everything you do. Things don't "just happen" in your life or your career. They are either consciously created by you, or they are unconsciously allowed by you.

TIPS OF THE MARKETING TRADE
In this section we will focus on the "how-to's" of some critical factors in the marketing/branding process such as:

Headshots
Resumes
Websites
Reels
Postcards
Social Media
Auditions
Self-Submission Casting Websites

Let's delve into the nitty-gritty of getting yourself out there in the best way as we cover each marketing channel in detail.

(Again, we are speaking from an actor's perspective, so artists in other mediums may need to translate the following topics.)

Headshots

Headshots are the most integral part of show business. They are your calling card and usually the first thing people see before they actually lay eyes on you. In most cases, a headshot is the *singular* thing a casting director may ever see until you actually get an audition. In many instances, headshots are the only way you will be asked to sing or dance if they decide to "type" at an audition. In all cases, they must be professional, honest, and *look like the person who is going to walk through the door*. If you are a redhead in your picture, you better be a redhead when you walk in the room. There is nothing a casting director (or anyone in charge) dislikes more than a person walking into an audition who does not remotely resemble the person in the headshot.

When you are a junior or senior in college, your school may bring in a professional photographer to take headshots for a discounted rate. Most performing arts colleges/universities bring in people who have experience and the end product is usually good. These shots should serve you for a few years, as you are a "newbie" in any city. That said, make sure to do your homework and know that your pictures are going to be in line with current headshot trends. Newbie or not, your picture has to market you exceptionally well. Please do not rush into a decision or pick someone simply because they are cheaper to work with. If you need to take time and budget for this investment it will be well worth it.

Christine: I did not get pictures in college, because I found a good photographer who only charged $200 for headshots in NYC. She came highly recommended from other actor friends at the time. Those shots were good for a few years, and I got more than my money out of them. Once I signed with an agent and joined AEA, it was time for new headshots. So I started shopping. Today, color headshots are the norm, but when I first started shopping around, the trend of color pictures was just beginning. I found a great photographer in Arthur Cohen (www.ArthurCohen.com) and loved what we came up with in my shoot. Because I did my research and chose a wonderful photographer, I used them for many years. Well worth it!

Finding the right photographer is crucial. You need to feel comfortable and at ease during your shoot. You don't want any tension, worries or stress at your session or your shots won't come out right.

There are few ways you can scope out photographers. At Reproductions, they have headshot photographer books. I would suggest looking through these and picking four to five photographers whose work you like. It's completely up to you and how you want to market yourself. There are many options and many photographers to choose from. After you have narrowed it down, call them and set an appointment to meet. This is a common practice; you are about to drop several hundred dollars on their service so if they won't meet with you, don't consider them. Brides don't just pick a photographer off the Internet and pray they shoot their wedding the way they want. You need to interview them and see the space they shoot in. Do you want natural or studio lighting? What backgrounds do they have available? Do you want to do some shots outside? Are their hair and makeup people reputable and do you like their work? There are many variables that go into your decision and different photographers click with different people.

Christine: For some reason, headshots are generally less expensive in LA, like half price less expensive. Many actors have actually flown out to LA to get their headshots taken because the price of their plane ticket and their session was still cheaper than getting them taken in NY. Plus they got a trip to the West Coast! Again, do your research. Cheaper certainly DOES NOT mean better. But if you were planning a trip to Los Angeles anyway, you can go to the beach one day and get new shots the next.

Again, this is an important decision and one to weigh carefully. Ask your friends whom they used, or if you have an agent or know a casting director who would help you, go ahead and ask them. They will have opinions on which photographers they like or don't like. Look at photographer's websites and see what pictures jump out at you, or if you were casting an imaginary show, whose pictures would grab your attention and make you call them in. Find out who took those shots and get in touch with that photographer.

Once you have interviewed all of your photographer candidates, it's time to narrow it down to one. Hopefully this will be an easy decision after you have spoken with them and gotten a feel for their particular style.

Now that your appointment is booked, what happens next?

Your photographer should give you a checklist and there will be guidelines to follow. We strongly encourage you to follow them! Here are a few basic guidelines that most photographers will give you:

- Don't get your haircut within two weeks of your shoot. You know the saying, "The difference between a bad haircut and a good one is two weeks."

- If you are going to have a facial treatment or skin procedure, do it two weeks ahead of time.

- Watch your tan lines if you are going to show some skin. (*Do not* get a tan or sit out in the sun the day(s) before your session.)

- Plan your outfits ahead of time. Make sure they are pressed and ready to go. Think about the backgrounds you are going to use and what colors complement them. If you plan this out beforehand, you will have that much more time to shoot.

- If you are doing your own hair and makeup, do a trial run ahead of time.

- Get lots of sleep and drink lots of water in the two weeks (at least one week) before your shoot.

- Do not drink any alcohol the night before your shoot - it will make your skin puffy.

- Bring music that inspires you.

Basically, don't do anything drastic or make any major changes that might affect your body, face, or overall being. Don't take any new vitamins, medication, etc., before your session, because they could bloat you or you could have an allergic reaction. You don't want anything to negatively affect your appearance. The only thing you might want to increase would be your workout routine so you have a radiant energy (and abs) coming into the shoot.

*A word on hair and makeup:** Most reputable headshot photographers have several artists they work with. These people are usually very good at their job. That doesn't mean you don't have final say in what they are doing with your face or your hair. It's *your* shoot, *your* pictures, and you need to feel comfortable.

With that said, if the makeup artist is going to put very dark eye makeup on you and you are a more natural-type girl, speak up. On the other hand, color shots generally require more makeup than you may normally wear. We believe that you should trust the makeup artists, because they do this every day. Keep in mind that the shots are digital, so you can see what you look like before anything is printed. You can ask them to not go as dark with the makeup initially and then add as you go along. It's always easier to add than to take away.

If you have the perfect shade of foundation that matches your skin exactly, by all means bring it, and the same goes for lipstick, blush, etc. The artist may try something similar or go in a little different direction because of the colors you are wearing or the lighting, so be open minded, yet true to yourself. Remember, there is always makeup remover (and digital photo retouching)!

Overall, hair and makeup can be a very touchy subject and one that can cause a lot of anxiety. Trust the artist. If you have difficult skin, again, trust the artist. They may have to use more foundation/concealer on you than you feel comfortable with, but go with it. Check out your digital proofs as you go along, and then make a decision. Most makeup artists are also really good at shading. They can make your nose a little thinner than it is, or accentuate your cheekbones, but not so much that it still doesn't look like you. You may be amazed at what they can do, and learn a few tips in the process.

**A word on retouching*

Joe: This particular topic has two schools of thought: to retouch or to not retouch. My opinion is that it is fine to get rid of a shadow, take the shine off a button on your shirt, or erase a stray hair that nobody caught during the shoot. However, I do not agree with getting rid of wrinkles, laugh lines, crow's-feet, etc. If you have a big problem with that, get Botox or do something that will correct whatever it is you think needs correcting. In my view, you are who you are, and when you walk in the room with laugh lines or wrinkles that they didn't see in your headshot, they are going to be annoyed, especially for on-camera work. Just be comfortable with who you are and look your natural best. Anything else is trying to market yourself as something you're not. Like we said before, the person who walks into the room should be the same person who is on that 8x10.

Just as in fashion, headshot photography changes and certain looks may be in or out. Do your research and find out what people want to see. The current trend seems to be more of an acting shot, like you were caught in a moment. Basically, it is not just a pretty picture of you. It tells a story or captures an emotion. Some casting directors like full body shots and some don't. Some like very close up and others don't. You can't please everybody for sure. But know this: A lot of casting directors are seeing your headshot on their computer screens where your picture is only a few inches high, or on mobile devices as they are out and about, where your picture is even smaller. Think about that in your session. Is your shot too far away to really capture your eyes or your essence? Would your shot stand out from 50-100 others as director is scrolling through deciding whom to see for the car commercial? These are important factors to consider during your headshot session as well as when choosing which picture(s) to go with.

Resumes

The biggest piece of advice we can give to artists is *don't lie on your resume*! You may think that saying you played Cosmo in "Singin' in the Rain" at so-and-so theatre with such-and-such director looks good on your resume. Who will ever know the difference, right? Wrong. This business is so small - everyone knows everyone, or knows someone who knows everyone. When you get caught in an industry lie you have basically ruined your relationship with that casting director or whoever figured out that you fabricated your resume. It is not worth it.

If you are just out of college and don't have a whole lot of working credits, so what? Your resume will go from being training-heavy in the beginning, with not as much experience, to eventually the complete opposite. Your continued training is always very important. You would be surprised how many people behind the table actually notice whom you are currently studying with as much as whom you have studied with in the past. The main point to remember is to keep it up-to-date, and *no lying!*

As far as the layout of your resume is concerned, there is no prototype or exact science. If you are completely at a loss as to how to set up your resume, check out other actors' resumes at auditions or on their websites. There is no copyright on resume formats, so if you see a format you like, go ahead and use it. If you are working with an agent or manager, they may prefer a certain format and they may also have letterhead/template you need to use.

The one thing that we personally like on a resume when we are auditioning people is ample white space. Try not to take up every available space on the page with ink. The eye needs a break and space to digest what it is seeing. Having some space on the sides and around your name is great because casting directors often like to make notes right on your resume. When they are seeing hundreds of people a day, they can make notes on the resume side and then flip it over and remember exactly who you are.

Christine: Another pet peeve is correct spelling. I have actually pointed this out to people I have auditioned, especially when I see someone's name on their resume and I know it is misspelled. For me, it shows a lack of precision. Attention to detail is very important and misspelling and improper grammar is unnecessary and unprofessional. Do your homework and you can avoid some potential embarrassment.

> *Consider this: If you are auditioning for a lot of TV and film, you may want to list on-camera credits first. You may eventually have two or three different versions of your resume depending on what medium you are going in for

Please make sure your resume is either printed on paper and stapled to the back of your headshot, or printed directly onto the back of your headshot. Please trim the paper to match the size of your headshot, so that there is nothing loose or hanging over the edges; this is one of the biggest mistakes and it shows a lack of know-how and professionalism. Also, use matte (not glossy) paper for your resume so that directors/creatives can write on it. You will not make a lot of fans behind the table if they cannot easily write notes directly on your resume. These suggestions may seem like common sense, but you would be surprised at what people hand to a casting director.

Keep your resume up-to-date and keep it professional. That is part of your job when it comes to seeing and being seen, especially if you want to present yourself in the best light and get in the audition room!

Christine: Joe and I both have forgotten to take pictures/resumes with us recently. When the vast majority of your submissions are digital, it is easy to do! In my case, I was going in for producers (a callback) for CSI: NY. They were putting me on tape and I didn't bring my picture and resume. I had been in for the casting director the day before and just assumed they would have my picture with them since it was a callback. There were many lessons learned that day. NEVER ASSUME ANYTHING and ALWAYS HAVE A PICTURE AND RESUME...ALWAYS. Thankfully, Joe was around the corner finishing his acting class and had the car with the extra pictures/ resumes I had put in there (I got that lesson right). I was saved in this instance, but I got lucky. Take this "school of life" lesson to heart...I didn't need the added stress on top of LA traffic!

Websites

Someone writing a book for artists ten years ago may not even have mentioned having a website. In today's market, having a website is more important than having a business card, especially for an actor. Think about it. What can a casting director assess about you from your business card? They can see what you look like (if your picture is on there), your phone number, and an e-mail address. Even a picture and resume, while useful, aren't "complete" unless there is a website included on them. A website is where you can really show off! You can have your acting and/or choreography reel on it. You can have pictures of you in character and performance clips. You can link or embed videos from YouTube of yourself performing in a cabaret or singing the National Anthem at Wrigley Field. The possibilities are endless. A casting director can see how well you sing, act, dance, and play the kazoo all from the comfort of his/her office!

Christine: A director friend of mine recently relayed a story about how he cast someone off of his YouTube videos. The actor couldn't make the callback and the director did some researching on the web. Luckily, the actor had put up some great stuff and lo and behold, they got the job!

To piggyback on the branding conversation, you can really control this aspect of your brand. You have the final say as to what people see, the order in which they see it, and what is available for view or download on your site. You don't necessarily have this with a Google search. So take advantage of it.

Just like your pictures and resumes, your website needs to be clean, professional, and a reflection of the real *you*. You don't have to break the bank on it, either. There are lots of options available that are inexpensive yet very effective. Shop around. Find sites that you really like, adapt what you like about the design, and make it your own.

Make sure to keep your website updated! Keeping buzz about you is important in this business. If a casting director checks out your site and you haven't updated it in six months, that's not very appealing. Work begets work, so brag a little! If you led a workshop at your university, that's great! Put a video up or blog about it. If you did a big industrial and have a copy of it, post it! You get the idea. (Note: adhere to all copyright laws, please!)

Joe: A quick technical note about websites. I've learned a ton from working with a top-notch web development company and the big thing I want to pass on is that search engines generally do not like sites built in Flash. (Geek alert) When the web crawlers (like the ones Google and other companies use) go out and scour the Internet they are reading sites and looking for text within the site. Flash, in simple terms, is an image/animation-based code language - most search engines can't read the text in a Flash-based site because they can't see it. (Also some Apple devices like iPhones can't read Flash.) As of now HTML code is still what the search engines can see and read the best. This all matters because if you want to be seen on the web, and that is the point of your site, then you need to build it in a format that will allow you to bump up on the search engine lists much faster and easier.

Keep your website easy to navigate and if you can, try to keep people on your site. What we mean is, avoid having pictures/videos that they have to leave your site to view. Use photo and video viewers/players that pop up right on your site. Once they view it and close that window, they are *still* on your site and becoming a huge fan of yours! If you lose them to another site, they may not come back. Make your site as "sticky" as possible - include lots of reasons for people to hang around, keep reading, and see all the wonderful things you have going on.

Since we are all Thriving Artists with lots happening, if you have a side business or a product to promote, add it to your actor site or create a separate site and link to it. If you are shooting headshots on the side or teaching Pilates, it is imperative that you have a website for that business. Plus, you can make money in your sleep. If you have written a book about how to cook on a budget, your book could be selling while you are auditioning. How's that for a good use of time? Ask yourself, when was the last time you opened a phone book? So why would you not put yourself and your business in the most visible place possible? The web is where it is all happening and you and/or your business need to be there.

Yet another advantage to having a website is that you never know who may want to advertise on your site.

Christine: When I tore my ACL, I found the blog of a woman who also had reconstructive surgery right around the same time. She sustained the injury doing karate. She is a black belt and a mother of two. Her writing style was funny and poignant and I found myself coming back to read it often. It turns out that a lot of other people did too and she now has quite a few advertisers paying her to promote their products or services because of the traffic to her blog. Currently she has Gatorade and Hotels.com. Not too shabby right? Talk about making money in your sleep!

The importance of a utilizing a website for your acting career or any other business venture cannot be overstated. If you are not on the web, then you practically don't exist. If it scares you, that's fine…just do what you need to do to get over it, and learn how to make use of this amazing marketing tool. Your career and brand may depend on it.

Reels

If you are an actor in any city across the country a reel is an absolutely critical piece of marketing material. Even for musical theater performers it can be a huge benefit to have one as well. A reel is a collection of your work to date that you are most proud of and want industry professionals to see, and it is a perfect place to continue to brand yourself. If you do not have any professionally shot material that can be edited down into a three- to five-minute reel there are several companies out there that will write original material for you and then go film it. Check out their work prior to hiring them and make sure the product looks like something that you would want to have out there as part of your marketing package.

If you are signed with an agent or manager, they might help you with putting your reel together. Some higher-end agencies will have reels produced in-house for their actors to maintain a certain "quality control" on the people they represent and how they are going to be marketed to casting directors and other industry professionals. Some casting directors will not even call you in for an audition if you do not have a reel they can view.

We are living in a digital world, and in our business, time is always an issue. Casting directors want to be able to sit at their desks, see your work online, and *then* decide if they want to bring you in for an audition. Your reel will save you time and it saves them time as well.

Another current trend is that casting directors don't want to view your entire five- or ten-minute reel to see all that you can do. We know you are fabulous. We know you are ridiculously talented...but time is money. What they want now is to have clips of your reel segmented into topics such as "comedy," "drama," "hosting" etc. Yes, you can still have your entire reel available, complete with intro music and cross fades, but much of the time *they only want to see what is relevant to the project at hand.* Sitting through 4 minutes and 30 seconds to get to the part they needed to see just ain't happenin' anymore; so, you need to cut your reel and make it look nice in little pieces, while at the same time having the entire reel available as well.

Postcards

Now that we have lived on both coasts, we can tell you that postcards in New York are good to have, and postcards in LA are imperative. This is how most casting directors want you to follow up with them. If you took a workshop with them a few weeks ago, and you recently landed a guest spot on NCIS, by all means, send them a postcard. If you have new headshots or are performing at the Hollywood Bowl/Joe's Pub/Don't Tell Mama, send them a postcard. But do not send them a postcard if you have nothing new to report, because it is a waste of their time and your money. Casting people want to know that you are out there in the field working and being pro active about your career. Since you are now officially a Thriving Artist, you will always have something to report!

As with auditioning, keep accurate records of whom you send postcards to and when. Do not inundate them every other week with every little bit of news but rather build two, three, or four juicy tidbits of news and do it every four to six weeks.

Here is a quick story from Leslie Becker, the author of *The Organized Actor®* and fellow Thriving Artist, about the effectiveness of postcards:

Leslie: I believe in keeping in touch with people in the industry. I believe when you do that consistently, it pays off. Particularly when you're starting out, getting your name and face out in the world consistently is extremely important. I diligently send out postcard announcements of the projects I'm working on. Even now, when most people use the Internet, I still use the mail. It's personal, it packs a punch, and even though it may go in the trash, it at least gets seen...unlike e-mail, where someone can see a subject and delete it before opening it. There was a theatre I wanted to work for very badly. I'd auditioned for them many times and always felt like they liked me but it never quite panned out. But I kept them on my mailing list, faithfully sending something every four-six weeks for a couple of years. On a random Thursday afternoon while getting ready to close the show I was in at the time, I got a phone call from the artistic director. "Hi, Leslie, we lost one of our performers for the last two shows of our season. We've always wanted to hire you and I have one of your postcards sitting right here on my desk and would love to offer you to take over the roles. Can you start on Monday?" It just so happened my current show was closing Sunday and I started rehearsal on Monday morning for one of the biggest theatres I'd ever worked for at the time. It was a huge jump in my career and was the first seed that led me to moving to New York City. I learned very early on, that even though you don't always get cast for the correct project, people do remember you if you remind them. Moral: Keep yourself on their desk.

Social Media

This was a topic that wasn't even relevant just a few years ago, but in today's market people can make their careers with the proper use of this marketing platform. This is an aspect of your business that needs to be updated on a very consistent basis, if not every day. There are people and companies out there that are experts on this topic and we have learned a great deal recently about effective use of social media. It is a FREE way to reach millions of people with your art; if you are intimidated by it, or don't understand it, now is the time to learn. Here are a bunch of tips that can enhance what you are already doing in the world of social media marketing:

Facebook: It is currently the Goliath of social media platforms, as we all know. Instead of using your profile to market your art, create a Facebook page dedicated to your art and your career and invite people to become your fans/followers. Professional people are more and more often going to Facebook and other outlets to "cyber-stalk" you. Your page can be the perfect place to put anything and everything about your career in one place. It is fine if you occasionally post about something personal, but if someone is researching you regarding a job, they don't want to sift through seeing that your dog recently got a haircut or that you just cracked the 100th level on "xyz-ville" and your digital city is booming. At that moment in time, they are very likely to not care...at all. Save the bulk of that for your personal profile and create a space for people to see you in the best professional light possible.

Create a Twitter account. It may seem like Facebook status updates are exactly like tweets, but they are not. Look at it this way. Facebook status posts can be much like you standing on a street corner with a megaphone. You can talk as long as you want and all but write a book in there. It's a place where you broadcast who you are, what you are doing, what your opinions may be about current events, etc. It is a great place to gather like-minded people together. Twitter, on the other hand, is much more like being at a cocktail party. It is a conversation. You only get 140 characters to work with, so writing an editorial on there just doesn't work. People tend to write questions, answer questions, and really engage with other users. It can give you more direct access to people and you can have some form of conversation with them there.

Create a LinkedIn profile. The reason we mention this one is because it is a platform that is solely dedicated to the networking of professionals. This is where decision makers and power players across all sorts of professions are more likely to "hang out." You can list your job experience, post your resume, and get endorsed by your peers. If you want to list all of your work experience, this is the place to do it.

Start a blog. This is where you can let your personality and passions really shine. You can blog about anything and everything that lights you up as a person and regarding your career. A blog is just a huge opportunity for you to share what it is you are about.

Regularity of updates/tweets. Consistency is a major factor in gaining "likes" and followers. If you don't know what to say then just get on there and respond to what you see. Share content that is in line with you and what you believe and want to share with the world (both personally and professionally).

Link your social media accounts to a central hub. There are a few good applications that let you do this. We like HootSuite. From there you can see, for example, your Facebook profile, Facebook page, Twitter account, and LinkedIn account. It is currently free to link up to five accounts (any more than five and you have to pay a monthly charge). The latter may be something you need if your business interests grow and you are managing a social media presence for all of them, but start with the free version for now.

Have all social media channels push back to your website. As we mentioned before, your website is the mother ship of your entire digital marketing world. Without it, all you have are a bunch of slivers shooting every which direction. On your website you can have everything in one place: pictures, videos, blogs, Twitter, and Facebook feeds. It's the concept of "all roads lead to Mecca," and Mecca is your website. When you send emails, it is your website link that you share at the bottom of your signature, not several different ones. Send a potential fan or employer to *one* place to learn about you. And then, of course, on your website you have links to all your various social media channels, but the lions share of the information is all on your site. A clean website with information that is easy to access will be greatly appreciated by those looking you up.

There are literally books upon books and classes upon classes available on the topic of social media marketing. The few tips above are, at best, just barely scratching the surface of how to effectively use this outlet. Wherever you are in your experience level with social media, we cannot urge you enough to start using it and put yourself through a "trial by fire" of sorts. Find a tutor, or a class, or just ask around for a good book and teach yourself if you have the time. Social media is a crucial part of your overall marketing strategy. Take advantage of it.

Joe: I was recently working with a casting director here in LA and learned an incredible lesson about the importance of social media. As soon as an actor that we all liked walked out of the room she immediately would turn to one of her assistants and say, "How many followers do they have on Twitter?" It seems crazy but it's true.

People in decision-making positions want to know you are bringing something to the marketing table. Are you bringing in a certain built-in fan base? All things being equal, if there are two actors who are perfect for the part and one has a huge following and the other doesn't, guess who is going to get the part?

Auditions

We placed this topic after the previous marketing tools because there is a loose hierarchy to how we ordered the list. The aforementioned tools are all equally necessary for professionals to market themselves effectively. Many times actors/singers/dancers think that if they just get in the audition room they can wow the creative team with their brilliance. Our point is that you may never see the inside of a big audition room without all the things we listed before in good working order. So make them important, give them thought, and take quality actions. You may find yourself in many auditions that were previously out of reach.

Jonathan Flom, our friend and author of *25 Secrets to Giving a Fantastic Musical Theatre Audition,* summed up auditioning in one sentence. In short, he says that, "as performers our *job* is auditioning!" What we are saying regarding that statement is that auditioning is, in many ways, what you have the most influence over. *You* control what you are going to sing, how prepared you are, what you look like, etc. Doing your "job" is going in there and knocking it out of the park. What happens after that is completely *not* up to you and therefore something you should waste no time trying to figure out.

We want to share some lessons we have learned "on the job" from years of audition experience in having some huge successes, and making a few mistakes along the way.

> Thriving Tip #1: **Do not think of an audition as an audition.**

Do not even think of an audition as a job interview, a tryout, or anything that implies you want or need anything from the people behind that table. You do not want approval, you do not want a job...you don't even want a pat on the head. You are not there to please anyone! You are simply there to reveal yourself, and your art, to the creative team, and this setting is a perfect opportunity for you to do that. Doing our job well means to simply give a great performance in the room and make everyone in there a new fan of yours, nothing more.

Does it sound odd to you that an audition is *not* to get a job? Let us explain. Once again it comes down to what your context of the audition is. If it is one of weakness and need, you'll never be at your best. People can smell desperation a mile away. If the context is of you being fully confident in what you do, and showing that confidence with zero attachment to what happens when you leave the room, then you will succeed every time; job or no job, callback or no callback. People are attracted to confidence like a magnet. (Note: We said confidence, not arrogance or entitlement...and there is a huge difference) Often as performers, we get conditioned into constantly seeking approval from others, and let's face it, more often than not, your fate as an artist is up to someone else's opinion. Think about it for a moment, and you will realize how insane it is to try to gain the approval of others, when you have no idea what they want. You have no control over what they are thinking, so stop trying to guess. Just go in the room and be you.

Treat the audition like a full-out performance, because this is where the magic happens. What is going through your head when you are on stage during a show? You're not (or shouldn't be) wondering, "Will the audience like me?" "How do I look/sound right now?" "Where are the reviewers sitting and what are they thinking?" So why on earth would you want to go into a room and have all that mental noise cluttering your head while you are performing?

You are at your very best when you are fully committed to the moment, and when nothing else exists except who you are, and what you are saying as that character. That is what you want to bring into the room, a fully realized and developed performance, not somebody singing through gritted teeth just hoping they will get passed on to the next round. If you perform well, if you are satisfied with the job you did when you leave, then you were successful. Everything else: the callback, the job, etc. are all up to elements far beyond your control.

A healthy amount of detachment from any desired result is absolutely necessary to get that result. We realize this may sound counterintuitive, but you have to release your grip on what you want for it ever to come to you.

Joe: I remember my first callback process for a Broadway show. It was for Beauty and the Beast *for the part of LeFou and I knew I was perfect for it. All I had to do was go in there and show them what I could do. I was working with someone at the time who had been in the show, and she coached me on the scenes and the song to help me prepare. When audition day came I was prepared in every way I thought possible, except one. I hadn't let go of what I wanted. I went in there and danced, and sang, and acted really well, but I was doing it all with the intention to "show them I could do it in the show" rather than just being completely in the room. I was auditioning to get a result, not for the joy of performing. There is a huge difference. Needless to say I didn't get the part, and quite honestly I can admit now that I wasn't ready for it yet. I hadn't learned how to let go. Fast forward a few years and I found myself at a chorus call for the biggest show of that time,* Hairspray. *The Broadway show had been running for a year and they were casting the first national tour. Everybody (and I mean everybody) wanted to be in it, including me. I wanted to do that show so much I could taste it. I had listened to the recording over and over and every time I heard it I would turn to Christine and say, "I have to do this show!" I would get chills just thinking about it. There were close to five hundred people there the day I auditioned, and only a few spots available in the show, so needless to say I was amped up. They brought us in the room fifty or more people at a time to learn the combination and then we got into groups of ten to do it for the creative team. Normally when you get put into smaller groups it's usually around four sometimes only two at a time. The dance combination was about thirty seconds long so, doing the math, that gave each of us about three seconds of time when Jerry Mitchell (the choreographer) would be looking at us. Three seconds?! REALLY?! Yes, really. I mean, they never said that outright, but watching the groups ahead of me dance and watching how long Jerry would take with each person, I kind of knew how long I had. So what was going through my head? Well, lots of things, but the mantra I kept saying over and over to myself was, "Let go...stay in the room and love what you are doing...let go...stay in the room and love what you are doing." The rest is history. I got kept all day. I got called back in about three or four more times...and then I got cast in the original touring company of* Hairspray. *I'll never forget getting the call from my agent telling me I booked it. It is one of the proudest moments of my career. And all while I was auditioning, each time I went in to sing or dance or read, I would make myself let go of anything that might or might not happen once I left the room. I didn't make myself stop caring, but I did make myself let go of it all. The more you want something, the more you have to let it go. Otherwise they will never see the love you have to give; they will just see someone trying to show off and get a job. Just love what you do... and let go.*

Thriving Tip #2: **Be prepared.**

You will hear this over and over throughout your career. Know your material forwards, backwards, upside down, and inside out. Do not go in the room with something that you learned just for that audition, *unless* you had plenty of time to coach on it and maybe even get to a piano bar and perform it live. If you are truly going to be at your best, you must be completely comfortable with your material. The audition already has enough variables—(room size, reverb, lack of reverb, a bad pianist, etc.) so be rock solid with what you are performing.

Christine: This was a hard lesson learned for me. I was still relatively new to New York and the Broadway audition scene when I started getting serious callbacks for the title role in Thoroughly Modern Millie. *In some cases, I had less than twenty-four to thirty-six hours to learn the material they gave me and come back in for the whole creative team. Did I work on everything? Sure I did. What I did not do was schedule time with my vocal coach, acting teacher, go see the show again that night - basically pull out all the stops and leave no stone unturned in my preparation. I left some room for error and although my callbacks were good, I didn't hit a home run. Looking back now, I remember feeling young, my comic timing not fully realized, and my nerves getting in the way at times. And this was in front of the original musical director, Michael Rafter and Jim Carnahan, the casting director... oh, to go back in time!—*

Try this:

A good exercise is to take anything that is new in your book (that you want to use in an audition) and go perform it in front of people. Go to a piano bar, hand your music to the accompanist, and sing it. We suggest that you record yourself doing the song at performance level, and get any nerves out about it being your first time. At the very least, you should have a voice teacher or coach listen to you doing it full out. The same goes for monologues. Get a group of your friends together and show each other your new material. Performing in front of your peers will surely be the most nerve-racking situation to put yourself into, but it's great practice. Performing in front of a bunch of strangers is a cakewalk after that!

Joe: I was getting deeper into auditions for Jersey Boys *(for the role of Frankie Valli) and was fresh off what is now known as "Frankie boot camp." I took one of the songs to a piano bar on 46th Street called Don't Tell Mama. I was extremely nervous going up to the microphone. I had never sung at a piano bar before, let alone doing a world-famous song. Christine was there as well as my good friend James T. Lane. I had them come and listen to me that night to pile on the adrenaline, so I had peers __and__ a live audience. If I could do it here, I could surely sing it well come audition time! Once it was over I had an amazing time! The audience loved it, sang along and a few minutes later called me up for an encore. I'm not saying that to brag. I'm saying it because you never know what it's going to feel like and how the audience will react unless you do it live with no safety net! I am 100 percent certain that I had better auditions because of that night. While I haven't been cast in the show yet, that is actually secondary to the fact that I was fully prepared when I walked in the room. I did my absolute best and left it all on the table. I want the same thing for you at every audition.*

Thriving Tip #3: **Choose great material.**

The material you choose should serve you and your talents perfectly. Remember, the point of an audition is for you to reveal yourself to the creative team, and your material should be your biggest ally in doing so. The audition is not to convince them or sell them on anything. As much as they are looking at your talent, they are also looking at *you*. The material you choose to perform should just be a tool in the audition process. Think of your material like a window into you: The bigger the window, the more of you they see, and that is a very good thing.

Now, that is not to say you should go into a Gilbert and Sullivan audition and sing them your favorite Beastie Boys tune just because it makes you feel good. Obviously you need to be intelligent about your choices and what you are going in for. What you choose does not have to be the exact fit for the show, but as long as it is in the same ballpark, you are OK. Sometimes in the audition breakdown, they will tell you exactly what they do or do not what to hear. We both appreciate this information because you are not changing your song at the last minute when the musical director comes out and says, "No Webber music today, please." The more information you have, the better.

In an odd way, finding good material for yourself can be one of the most mind-numbing tasks you will face. Finding music/monologues/scenes that have not been overdone, are appropriate for you/the show, and will reveal the best you have to offer is a tall order. The bottom line is to do your research and choose material wisely.

As we mentioned earlier, Broadway (or whatever your art form) is a marketplace, so you need to constantly be aware of what is *in* that marketplace. What sorts of shows are being produced? In what style are they being written? Pop? Classical? Jazz? Country/Western? Now, look at yourself as a product that is to be "sold" in that marketplace. If you have a variety of material in your audition book, and that material is appropriate for what is out there, you are on the right track once again.

Also, your audition material has to light you on fire! If you aren't looking forward to performing it, then it's time to find new material!

Finding new material is a process that never ends. Because you keep changing with age, and the marketplace keeps changing, you will always find yourself updating and periodically cleaning out your book. That is always a good thing because it keeps you fresh.

Thriving Tip #4: **Be honest with yourself.**

Know what you are right for. Take a good long look in the mirror. Be brutally honest with yourself about what you can do and what your limitations are. Ask a few trusted friends, colleagues, or mentors to give you their "gloves off " opinion. It may sting a bit, but at least you'll have a better idea where your holes are so you can start working to fill them in.

Be truthful with yourself as to where you are, but never sell yourself short as to what you are capable of. Continue to develop and work on what you are already good at, but always, *always*, keep working and improving in areas where you are weak. The more you can do, the more doors will open for you.

The reality is that you truly never know what they are looking for, so do not take yourself out of the running for something too early. If you think you aren't quite right according to a casting breakdown, but know in your gut that you can bring something new and make the creative team see things in a different way, then by all means get your butt to that audition!

There are many excuses people use to not go to an audition: You are "tired from working" the night before. There will only be a "casting assistant in the room" so why bother? Or one of our favorites, your friend told you "the lead is already cast." Unless it says in the breakdown that the role is already cast, no one knows that for sure. People turn down contracts all the time. People get sick, or other opportunities arise. The point *is that you will never get the job unless you are in the room.*

Leslie: I'm someone who loves to audition! I believe that the more you go on, the more opportunities you have to get cast, and the better you get at them. I have a commitment to myself to NEVER go more than two weeks without going to an audition. Sometimes there are slow periods though when you feel like there aren't any auditions for projects that you are right for. This happened a few years back. I woke up one morning and realized I hadn't had an audition for almost two weeks, so instead of wallowing about it, I looked to see what was auditioning for that day. All I could find was a singers' call for some show I was not remotely right for. But I had a commitment to never go two weeks without auditioning, so I went. Everyone was singing their sixteen bars and coming out of the room quickly. Then it was my turn. I sang a full song and no one stopped me. I sang another full song and no one stopped me, and then I got a very kind thank-you. I knew they liked me but I also knew I wasn't really right for the show. To me, that didn't matter. I held myself to my commitment of never going two weeks without an audition. A few days later I got a call from my agent to go in for a project I'd never heard of, and when I walked in the audition room, there was the music director from the chorus call I had attended. "Hi, Leslie, you came in for me the other day and I thought you'd be perfect for this project." I sang three full songs for him and twenty minutes after I left I got the call from my agent that I'd booked the job. This job ended up being one of my most satisfying theatrical experiences to date, and I booked it simply because I showed up. Moral: You can't get cast in your living room. Go. Just Go. Leslie Becker is the author of The Organized Actor®.

Thriving Tip #5: **Audition in good faith.**

If you know with absolute certainty ahead of time that you are either unavailable or unwilling to take a job you are auditioning for, then by all means *do not go!* It is very rude (not to mention unprofessional) to go audition, show them something wonderful, and when you get the offer, tell them no. It is a waste of their time and frankly, it may anger the casting director. You may think that you are getting ahead because you are "being seen" by that casting office and creative team, but if word gets back to them (and believe us, it can and will) you might find yourself going out on fewer auditions for that casting office. Now, that is *not* the same as choosing one job over another when several come through. If that is the case, congratulations, you have more work than you can handle! Auditioning in good faith and being up front with what your schedule allows will pay you huge dividends for your reputation (Brand) with industry people in town.

Joe: I was in the Broadway production of Disney's The Little Mermaid *when something came across my desk that I really wanted to do. I got called in to audition for the role of Igor in the national touring production of* Young Frankenstein. *What a wonderful role and what a fantastic opportunity to take a step forward out of the ensemble and into the roles I always wanted to play. At the time Christine was pregnant with our son and was going to deliver just a few months after the tour would have left town. That meant she would have finished her third trimester without me, I would have come back for the delivery, and then jumped back out on the road after only a few short days or weeks. I knew immediately that I wasn't going to miss ANY of that - not a chance in the world. But I did want to be seen by Susan Stroman and the creative team. I ran the idea by our resident dance director at The Little Mermaid, Tara Young, who had worked very closely with Stroman for several shows. I told Tara that there was no way for me to take the job but asked her if I should still go in and audition. She told me nothing makes Susan Stroman angrier than people who waste her time, and that going in knowing I couldn't take the job would have been a huge mistake. So, I let it go and never auditioned. I knew in my gut it was the right thing to do, and my conversation with Tara reconfirmed that feeling. I hate having my time wasted as well, and I wasn't about to waste someone else's time. Avoid the trap of being seen at all costs...it may cost you more in the long run.*

Thriving Tip #6: **Be available.**

When you are in the room, *be in the room.* If they like you and have you do something again, listen to their directions! Don't talk, don't interrupt, don't agree with them while they are talking, and definitely do not say, "I know." Just stand there, listen, breathe, and make yourself available. They are not spending precious time on you because they think you suck! If you don't understand something, it is OK to ask for clarification, and then do your best to apply the directions you were given. Always remember that nothing is personal, even though we as artists often tend to take it that way. The creative team has a job to do and they are seeing if you have what they need for the show. Make it easy for them by being fully present in the room. They will love you for it.

> Thriving Tip #7: **You are rarely auditioning for just one thing at a time.**

There will be auditions where you will walk out on cloud nine, and there is no greater feeling! We hope you experience it often. You will swear up and down that you "nailed that audition" and the contract is being printed even as you call your best friend to tell him or her all about it. But, oops, no job! How can that happen? Well, there are a million reasons and all of them have absolutely *nothing* to do with you! Either there weren't enough equity contracts, or non-equity contracts, or the director/musical director/choreographer wanted someone they knew…the list goes on and on. So you throw your hands up and wonder why you put yourself through it.

If you can give that great of a performance, be perfect for the role, and *still* not get it, why continue to run full-speed into a brick wall? There are two answers to that question:

1. The first answer is because that's your job! Nobody said putting your heart and soul on a platter was going to be easy or that it guaranteed you a callback or a part in a show. It just guarantees that you are giving 100 percent and in that, you need to find a large measure of satisfaction. You have to be willing to run into that brick wall just as fast the next time, even though your head might still hurt from the time before. Remember, this is about marketing, selling, and branding yourself, and how you handle rejection and tough times will speak volumes about you. Best to be known as the person who always gives everything they've got no matter what.

There is a quote that says: **"A sale is not something you pursue; it's what happens when you are immersed in serving your customer."** How very appropriate for show business as well. That is why we say auditions are *not* about getting a job. They are about doing a "presentation of your product to the board of directors." As long as you are focused on them and solving their casting *problem* with your performance solution, the "sale" of you getting the job will be an easy choice for them to make.

2. The second answer is that there is usually a silver lining. They will remember you next time! You made an amazing impression on that whole creative team and next time you are in the room with them, you are more likely to get a callback/cast because of your previous work. Anyone can be a flash in the pan, but consistency generally wins out in the end. Continually show them good, interesting, and intelligent work, and the likelihood of booking a job will skyrocket. Remember that even though you didn't get the first job, the creative team may have been sitting there talking about their next project and how you could be perfect for it.

Joe: New York City Center Encores! was *doing a production of* Gypsy *with Patti LuPone, and it had been a show I always wanted to do. I went to an open call where everyone around me looked, at least to my eyes, much younger than me, and therefore more likely to get the job. It was one of the few times in my career when I honestly thought about packing up my stuff and going home, because I figured there was no way I was getting past the first cut! But I decided to stay and give it my best because who knows, right? Well, because I was already cut in my mind, my only concern was giving a good audition and having a great time in the room. I didn't have any thought of actually getting the job. And of course, guess what happened: I got a callback! I got <u>several</u> callbacks! I got right down to the end for the part of Yonkers, a nice featured role in the ensemble for a very high-profile job. As the callback process continued my hopes got higher each time, but ultimately I did not land that job. Discouraged as I was, I still felt great about my work. I had given them everything I had to give, and that was all I could do. The rest was up to the mix-and-match game of casting directors and creative types. Just a short while later I ran into the associate choreographer, who made it a point to tell me that everyone loved what I did and was pulling for me, but it was only the director who couldn't see me in the show. So an audition I almost left turned out to be a job I almost landed. That may sound like a net gain of zero, but it doesn't work like that in show business. I found an ally in the associate choreographer and I also have an ally in that casting office, because I had such a good showing. Shortly after that process concluded I was called in for several other big projects they were casting. The whole process is much easier when you know that they are on your side. I was easily getting into auditions that I knew other people were struggling to get into, and it was a time in my career when I knew I had taken another nice step forward in being known about town.*

Auditions can be the most exalting or the most terrifying event in a performer's life. If you are prepared, have good material, are the consummate professional, and just focus on the moment at hand rather than the outcome, you will be far ahead of those around you.

Self-Submission Casting Websites

A book written just a few years ago may not have mentioned these sites. However, nowadays, an artist can get a lot of exposure and work because of sites like ActorsAccess.com and LACasting.com just to name a few. This can be helpful for artists without representation. There are a few things to keep in mind when submitting yourself on these sites:

1. The quicker you submit, the better. If a casting director puts out a notice for a print job, she will get thousands of submissions within a few hours. She can usually find what she needs, on that first day of submissions, so if you aren't checking these sites regularly and submitting quickly, you are missing the window of opportunity.

2. Have your material ready and available. Make sure your reel is available to view. Multiple pictures are also handy. If you often play a cop or a detective, a shot of that can get you in the room. If you dance or practice yoga regularly, a professional shot of you doing anything athletic can put you in the running for print or commercial jobs needing specialties.

3. Tell the truth. Like your resume, you won't make any friends or do anyone any favors if you say you can ice skate, get booked for the job, and you show up on set and are not as proficient as you led them to believe. Nothing will put you on the "do not call" list faster than this.

4. Submit for things you are going to take. If you know you won't work for free or you have a conflict that you won't change, don't dangle the carrot in front of them. Honesty is the best policy.

Last Thoughts on Seeing and Being Seen
Be Well Rounded, Be Real
Have you ever met someone in this business who can only talk about *the business*? We are all for pop culture and being informed as to who was nominated for what award, but please be able to talk about other things! Pick up a copy

of the *Wall Street Journal* or *Businessweek* and open up your horizons. Take a Bikram yoga class. Watch a baseball game from start to finish and memorize some of the players' names. In short, do something *not* associated with your profession. By exposing yourself to different experiences, you never know what extra connection you can make when building your relationships with industry people. Remember, industry people are also people with lots of interests outside their industry. Be curious about everything and *get out of your comfort zone*. If it scares you, do it.

Christine: If you know me, you know that I am a sports fan! A big one and Philly fan to boot. I joined the national tour of The Best Little Whorehouse in Texas, *starring Ann-Margret, in the fall of 2001. Football season was just starting. Luckily the crew guys were also sports fans and there was usually a TV showing the games on Sundays somewhere in the backstage area. Little did I know that our star, the lovely and incomparable Ann-Margret, was also a sports fanatic. She loves the Oakland Raiders. When she found out I was such an avid football fan, she invited me to watch the games in her dressing room with her in between shows. We would order in and she, her husband, Roger, their dog, Missy, and I would watch the games. This became a ritual for us for the entire season all the way through the Super Bowl. These are memories that I will never forget with an icon from the stage and screen. No other woman in the cast shared our love of football quite as much and because I had other interests outside the industry I made a lifelong friend. We still chat to this day about football.*

Resist the temptation to give someone your resume every time you open your mouth!

Having other interests outside your art has a grounding effect and will plug you into the world at large. Some of these interests might even pay you…but we will cover that later in our section on money.

Here are four reasons why having varied pursuits is ultimately a good thing for your career:

1. If you have a mediocre audition, it will not ruin your entire day, because you have something else positive to occupy your mind. Perhaps you have to run to a reading of a new show you wrote, or you are on your way to a class on stock

market investing. You will not have time to obsess over what you wore, how you sounded, or what it meant when the director shifted in his seat while you were singing (maybe he had gas? You'll never know!). Staying busy keeps you moving forward, and sometimes that is the best thing. Breathe. Do. Learn. Repeat.

Christine: Our friend Allison recently had a callback for producers for a series regular on a pilot. She prepared very diligently, met with her coach, knew the material backwards and forwards and gave an amazing callback. Everyone in the room was laughing; she did her job and won the room! She could have sat around and agonized over every little detail such as what she felt went right, what could have gone better, etc. But she couldn't because she had to meet with her realtor about her upcoming closing date on a rental/vacation property. Not only did she give a stellar audition, but she is also creating income in a powerful and creative way. Thriving indeed!

2. You will not reek of desperation. Trust us, desperation is like bad body odor; you may not be able to smell it on yourself, but everyone around you can! Remember those wallflowers at school dances, with deer-in-headlight eyes, scanning the crowd looking for anyone to ask them to dance? That is how a desperate person looks in the audition room. It is *not* attractive and it actually makes the people behind the table feel bad for you (which is an ineffective way to market yourself for sure!).

3. You'll be letting go and creating space. Have you ever noticed that after a long period of working toward something, that as soon as you stop obsessing over it, it comes to you? For instance, couples desperate to have a baby, after trying for months, finally decide to go to the adoption center to start that process, and lo and behold, two weeks later they find out they are going to have a baby of their own! Releasing that stressful energy of "gripping at" or *needing* something to happen always makes room for it to come to you. If you are constantly seeking, chances are you aren't finding. You have to make space for what you want so it can manifest. Continue to do your work. Work incredibly hard at what you want, and then let it go so it can come to you when the time is right.

4. Having a lot going on will also serve you well in social settings. Nothing will damage your brand more than being known as socially awkward or as a "shop-talking drone" who can't possibly have a conversation about anything else.

Having varied interests helps you be interesting! Another terrific skill to master is the art of asking great questions. People generally love talking about themselves or their work, and you can learn a whole lot by just listening. It's a balancing act. Of course you want to share and join in the conversation, but be mindful not to dominate it. Sure, ask lots of questions, but do not make people feel like the FBI is grilling them for information.

As we said above, just be *well rounded, real, and comfortable in your own skin.* In addition to all the tips, tricks, and techniques we offered on marketing and branding, this will serve you not only in your career, but throughout your entire life as well.

Chapter 5 – Focus On: Relationships
The Art of Networking

"There is no such thing as a 'self-made' man. We are made up of thousands of others. Everyone who has ever done a kind deed for us, or spoken one word of encouragement to us, has entered into the makeup of our character and of our thoughts, as well as our success"
- George Burton Adams

"The real winners, those with astounding careers, warm relationships, and unstoppable charisma, are those people who put it all out there and don't waste a bunch of time and energy trying to be something or someone they're not. Charm is simply a matter of being yourself. Your uniqueness is your power."
– Keith Ferrazzi, author of Never Eat Alone

Let's take a look at what you think of right away when we mention "networking." If you have a good reaction to it, great! If it makes you sick to your stomach or breathe a sigh of annoyance, by all means do some internal digging. Be sure to check all the shadows and make sure you are not hanging on to a negative feeling simply because it is comfortable. *Beware the conditioned mind!* Choose a positive context and attitude toward building your network, and then go out and create it.

The longer you are in this business, the more your relationship-building skills will become as important as how well you can sing, dance, act, paint, sculpt, etc. What do we mean? Have you ever heard the expression, "It's not *what* you know, it's *who* you know?" Very often it is true. A lot of people dislike this part of the game, but it is hugely important, so get used to the idea of having to do it. Where people go wrong is in how they perceive the meaning of the word "networking." This word can often get the same reaction as the word "selling," connoting being disingenuous or slimy in some way. This negative reaction goes against your inner principles of being honest and true in your relationships with other people, so you don't even like thinking about "networking." The rub of the situation is that we all need people to be on our side. We all need industry people who are in powerful positions to know us, like us, and go to bat for us when needed. The question becomes, "How do we balance the two worlds of needing a great network, and yet creating it in a way that feels good and is in line with our core values?" In the next section we will cover that in detail, starting with making a shift in context, and then adding all the "how-to's" to make it fun and effective.

Joe: I like to think of networking as nothing more than making friends and then tending to and deepening those relationships. If you like people, it's easy to do. I look to find something that genuinely connects me to the other person on some level. It could be anything: playing video games, the love of different whiskies, playing poker, where they are from, if we know the same people...whatever the case may be, I look for those connections between us. I am fascinated by people, their stories, and what makes them tick. The more I learn about someone, the greater the chance I have to relate on many levels. In my personal life or if I'm in an interview with a casting director who can have a huge influence over my career, it's all the same. People are people; you just have to enjoy the process.

Christine: There is a saying in gambling that "It's better to be lucky than good." Often I think that directly applies to show business. Everyone reading this can come up with a few people who seem to have the best luck in the world and, by your estimation, only average talent; yet they consistently work more than some people who are virtuosos. Why is it that some performers seem to follow around a certain director or choreographer from project to project? Or, why are the same musicians always in the Broadway orchestra pits? They got themselves the job either by being lucky, good, or both, and then cultivated and maintained a relationship with those who can hire them. They made a meaningful connection and it paid off down the road.

The skills of building your network are not to be taken lightly. We are sure you are getting that by now. Here are our top ten tips on the topic of networking effectively:

TOP TEN NETWORKING TIPS, SKILLS AND GUIDELINES

Christine's acting teacher in college gave her senior class two rules to live by in this business. One of them fits right in with our top ten, and is in the number-one slot for a reason:

1. Don't be a bitch. (Basically, be a nice person.)

This rule is our favorite. It is an absolute staple for effective networking and just about everything in life. If you haven't already figured it out, it *is* a small world. New York may be one of the biggest cities on the planet, but you may run into someone you know every single day, simply walking down the street. Artist communities are extremely small and word gets around fast. If you are hard to work with, you may find yourself unemployed more than you would like.

Now, if you *must* gossip or complain, and all of us do at some point, you should use the ten-block rule at a minimum. What we mean is, don't talk about how someone at an audition pissed you off while you are still at the Actors' Equity building or sitting at a Starbucks in Studio City. The odds are very high that someone within earshot knows of whom you speak. The rule we employ is simply this: wait until you are home to kvetch! We have heard horror stories about actors waiting for the elevator on the way to an audition and making snide comments about the casting director of the project they are about to go in for. Little do they know, that casting director's assistant is standing right there and heard the whole rant. Walls, elevators, streets…they all have ears. So mind your manners and your mouth when you are in hotspots for industry people.

Christine: I had a callback for 42nd Street *on Broadway a few years ago. I had made it past a few rounds and now had to audition in front of Jay Binder himself, of Binder Casting. It was around 9:30 a.m. and I was in the elevator with a man I had never met before. Frankly, I felt a bit tired. After all, 9:30 is early for us artists! Luckily, I didn't say a word. I didn't complain about hating mornings and particularly auditioning before noon. When I walked into the audition room, guess who was behind the table? Yep, the man I rode with in the elevator! I gave a great performance and he got to see me at my best. Unfortunately, I didn't get the job that day, but it wasn't because I had put my foot in my mouth. I can live with that.*

Being a nice person needs to be a golden rule that you live by, and not just to people you deem "worthy," but to everyone. There is no such thing in your career, or life for that matter, as an unimportant person. We are not advocating that you try to be everyone's best friend. That's impossible. We are not even saying you will be, or should try to be, especially close with more than a handful of people. What we *are* saying is that it is of the utmost importance to treat *everyone* who crosses your path with respect. We believe in energy and in karma...what you give is what you get and that counts on all levels. You just never know whom you are talking to. Big cities become small towns very quickly and word spreads like wildfire. If you have a stellar reputation your life will be much easier.

Oh, and in case you were wondering...the second thing Christine's teacher told her was to look out for number one because nobody else will. (Thanks, Patrick!)

2. Keep in touch.

If you think that any artist who is at the pinnacle of their craft did it alone, you are sorely mistaken. They had great teachers, grad programs, friends, family, associates, and people they met at dinner parties who helped shape their path to the top. Most importantly, they *cultivated* these relationships over time. No meaningful relationship happens overnight.

Christine: After I tore my ACL on the national tour of My Fair Lady, *I knew that getting back into the swing of things was going to be challenging. I found out first-hand that the recovery process is sometimes more a mental challenge than a physical one. Auditioning for the first few months after my injury was near impossible, and I was getting antsy. I knew I needed to get back on the stage and soon. Luckily I had maintained a good relationship with the wonderful artistic staff at Beef and Boards Theatre in Indianapolis. I had played the title role in* Thoroughly Modern Millie *and they welcomed me back anytime. I was looking online and noticed they were doing* The Sound of Music *starting nine months after my surgery. I had always wanted to play the role of Maria and it seemed a perfect re-entry into eight shows a week after a major injury. Using my networking skills (and my agent), I got the job. It is a charming and wonderful place to work, and it eased my mind as I transitioned back into performing.*

The term "cultivating relationships" can sound good, but can also be a bit daunting if you don't know how. Meeting someone new is like bringing home a new plant. Most people think growing their network is an event and not a process, but the complete opposite is true. It takes constant care and attention to make that new plant grow, and your relationships are no different. You wouldn't bring a new plant home, water it once, and then come back months later expecting it to have grown, would you? Yet artists do that all the time with people they meet in the industry. Devote some time and energy and your personal and professional life will be better for it. Here are some ideas for you as you build and cultivate your growing network:

- Once you have made contact with someone new, nurture the relationship with a phone call, email, or postcard once a month.

- If you want to turn a new contact into a *friend*, work for two face-to-face meetings outside of a professional setting.

- Put your contacts into categories on your phone/computer:
  Personal (i.e., good friends and social acquaintances)
  Choreographers
  Directors
  Cast mates by the show (i.e., people not in your "personal" category)
  Aspirational contacts (i.e., people you would like to get to know or have met briefly and want to build a better relationship)

- Use the "A, B, C" system to determine how and when to contact each person on your networking list:

  A – Relationships that have not been solidified should be contacted with at least three to seven forms of direct communication. Keep a note on the last time you made contact with them and how. Switch up between e-mails and calls and shoot for once a month to once every three weeks.

  B – The "touch base" people. People you already know well. You can make a quarterly call or e-mail and include in mass e-mails about your career.

  C - People you do not know well and are unable to devote any significant energy to contacting. Perhaps you met in passing, and they ended up in the address book. Connect to this group once a year.

Whenever you are reaching out, always try to make the message as personal as possible. Keep in mind and mention things that you spoke about or interests that you share so they have a mental anchor for you. Stay consistent with your relationship-building efforts and know that it is a marathon, not a sprint. It's also a process that never ends, so quickly make it part of your lifestyle so you can enjoy the ride and the growth.

This may all seem like a lot of work, and it can be, but do it well and your career may take leaps and bounds just by virtue of your being known by more people. You can never know what contact in your network will create an opportunity or just lead to a wonderful experience you may have otherwise missed. We have been to sporting events, awards show after-parties, opening nights, and screenings…all because of the quality of our relationships.

3. Generosity first.

As we said before, networking should never seem like a negative thing, nor should it be thought of as a one-way street only going *your* direction! As of this moment, we want you to stop thinking from a self-centered standpoint. We know that artists (especially actors) get a bad rap sometimes, because we have to be so focused on our product and ourselves. This focus can be perceived as selfish, but that is not the case at all when building your network. A Thriving Artist understands that a professional must network as a means to grow. Networking is a "*give* and take," so while taking, the artist is also giving, and networking becomes selfless rather than selfish!

Start from the thought of "What can I do for them?" rather than "What can they do for me?" It changes every interaction dramatically. If they have a problem, hear it as a chance to practice a sort of altruism where you immediately think, "I need to find a solution." If you don't have any personal advice, the solution may come from simply asking yourself, "How can my network of friends and contacts help this person?"

"You can't live a perfect day without doing something for someone who will never be able to repay you."
- *John Wooden*

4. Be on good terms with everyone.

This is just a good rule to live by no matter what your career. For artists, every single person you meet is important. That person may become a fan, lead you to other fans, become an influence on your career, or possibly lead you to someone who is an influence on your career. You just never know. You may get a surprise one day, when someone you worked with or met in passing is sitting on the other side of the audition table! What they remember about you, how you handled yourself, how you treated other people, etc., will definitely matter.

Joe: I was in between jobs in NYC when an audition for a replacement in Disney's The Little Mermaid *came across my path. I knew several of the cast already from working with them in* Hairspray*. One of those people in particular was Jason Snow. He was our dance captain on the* Hairspray *tour and then got transferred to Broadway shortly after I did. After I had been in callbacks for Mermaid I had a pretty good feeling about my chances for booking that job. It didn't take very long at all from my final callback to the phone call with the offer, and I was thrilled to join the cast. One day backstage I was talking about my audition/callback experience with Jason and all he said was something to the effect of "They [Disney] did their homework on people" before casting them. Then he gave me a wry smile, letting me know that when they asked him about me, he had put in a very good word. I still think to this day I owe a lot of my getting that gig to Jason. Thanks pal.*

5. Take names and do your homework.

Great achievement is always preceded by great preparation. Have a goal and map out the most important players in your specific field, and have a date of when you would like to connect with them. As the saying goes, if you aim at nothing, you will surely hit it, and the same holds true for building your network. Know who you want in your network and then bring them in!

Now, if you do know exactly whom you are going to meet on a given day, you had better know more about them than just their name. It seems like it would be common sense, but all too often people lose a chance to make a genuine connection because they didn't do their homework. Search on Google, IMDB, or other industry-specific databases and learn about who you are going to meet.

Joe & Christine: Our LA agent recently set up an intimate Q & A with one of the industry's top commercial casting directors, Danielle Eskinazi. We didn't know if we were going to get any one-on-one time with her but we still prepped as if we might. Joe drove down and while we were in the car, we went over the questions we might ask her in the Q & A session. Christine then brought up her website and read her bio. She frequently leads workshops for actors and teaches often at the Stella Adler Conservatory. Since we also teach workshops all around the country, and have contacts at Stella Adler, these could be our connection/common ground with Danielle. When doing our homework on new people we like to look for things that are as far outside the industry as possible. We find it keeps the conversation flowing easily and it's not just "shop talk." We both felt much better about meeting with a heavy hitter knowing a bit about her and what we could talk about. Ultimately we didn't end up having any one-on-one time with her, but we did practice the discipline of doing our research so in that, we succeeded. Joe has since connected with her several times on Twitter, which is one of her preferred communication methods, and we have a feeling our relationship will continue to grow. Good stuff indeed.

There are a million different ways to learn about people and what they are doing, so take advantage of that information and have it in your back pocket. You'll have the opportunity to turn what could be a forgettable encounter into a memorable and genuine experience. It's worth the effort!

Another point on names: You are going to meet people and not know who they are beforehand. That is fine. What is *not* fine is forgetting their name seconds after you hear it. If you find that this happens to you, it probably means you are not fully present in that moment. If you are not present in the moment, your lack of attention and focus is immediately evident. When that lack of focus and sincerity comes through it can appear that you are being opportunistic, and that is certainly something you do not want. We are emphatically telling you to *be in the moment, pay attention, and actively listen*. That will show your sincerity and your interest in the other person and make your encounter much more enjoyable and memorable.

Joe: Remember my story about winning at the name game? Well, here is how I did it. A trick I learned some time ago that has helped me remember names is the rule of three. Say that person's name three times throughout the conversation while looking them in the eye, and you are much more likely to remember it. Try the following:

Friend: "Joe, meet my friend Sam. Sam is the director of XYZ show up at ABC playhouse."

Joe: (simply repeat the name) "Sam? (Look him in the eye and extend your hand for a handshake.) Hey, Sam, it's nice to meet you. How are you doing?"

Right away you have said his name twice and it was completely natural. From this point, let the conversation flow as it normally would and then at the end, use his name one more time as you are saying good-bye. As an insurance policy you can silently repeat his/her name to yourself once or twice while they are talking. If by chance you have forgotten it, just own up to it. It's much better than trying to fake it or worse yet, seeing them again and not remembering. Names are magic! Remembering and using names in conversation lets the other person know that you are fully engaged and interested in what they have to say, and it creates a better rapport in less time. Trust me. I had to learn this one the hard way; after meeting someone repeatedly and asking his name at each encounter, he finally called me out on it and said, "Joe, I've met you four times!" Needless to say I was embarrassed and it motivated me to get much better at the name game.

6. Follow up or fail.

What is the point in meeting people and putting in all this effort to grow your network, if you aren't going to follow up and make them a part of your life in some way? We like the practice of following up twenty-four to forty-eight hours after meeting someone new. A good habit is to cite something specific about your encounter with them that you appreciated or learned. It is an acknowledgment of your encounter and the fact that you are specifically recalling a part of the conversation and taking the time to follow up. This shows once again that you were genuinely listening to what that person had to say.

What you do after your initial follow-up depends on what level or capacity you want to know that person. Is this person a potential business contact, or someone you want to know on a regular (and possibly personal) level? As mentioned earlier, you can go as far as creating lists and setting reminders to reach out to people on a monthly, quarterly, or yearly basis. Whatever you choose, make sure you are consistent and genuine. Be clear and specific with yourself on why you want to build this relationship. *Build a human connection first*, and any sort of business connection will flow from there. Of course there are no guarantees in this regard, but having a human connection first is always the best place to start before any other sort of relationship follows.

Christine: We have done numerous Thriving Artists workshops all across the country. I think I can count on one hand, maybe two the number of students who follow up with us on a regular basis. Out of hundreds of students, five or six keep us on their mailing list, send us postcards, and/or shout out on social media. Believe me, when a casting director or choreographer asks me for a referral for a job, and they often do, I would recommend those few first.

7. Become genuinely interested in other people.

The more you enjoy people, the better you will be at building your network. The more you learn about the person, the more meaningful the conversation can be, and whatever the resulting connection will likely be a deeper one. Things that people are generally always able to talk about are their families or where they are from, how they found their current occupation, what they do for recreation, and money or the stock market. These may seem like mundane topics, but they are great places to start if you find yourself at a conversational loss. Share something personal with someone and they will be inclined to share in return. This is very much common knowledge, but worth stating here: At first it is always best to avoid conversations on politics or religion. If you do venture down this land mine-filled path there are two things to consider. One is that you are secure enough in your relationship that if you differ greatly on a topic it will not damage your relationship. The second thing to consider is that you are 100 percent sure you both *agree* on a political/religious topic before you start talking about it. Making assumptions can sometimes do a lot of damage to a relationship. Stick to the beaten path at first and be mindful of where the conversation leads.

Also, find out what motivates that person to get up in the morning. What is their "why" for doing what they do? Is it the desire to make a lot of money? Is it the need to find true love? Or is it a calling to make a difference in the world? Whatever it is (usually one of those three) find out and then speak to that person on this level. The conversation will be organic and you will find yourself with a growing network not just of new business contacts, but with new friends, all simply because you took the time to listen and *connect.*

Christine: One of my go-to moneymaking jobs when I am not acting is catering. Out here in LA we are usually working in people's homes. Often we are in star's homes. Some people might become weirded out by being this close to them and I admit, there have been a few people who have rattled me. This is mainly because I admire them and their work and am a huge fan myself. But how I keep the conversation easy, flowing and NEVER about show business (which is a huge no-no), I approach them as a parent. Most of them have kids too and it makes them and I human. Anyone who has kids, from the biggest stars to stay-at-home moms can always and easily talk about their children.

> **"You can be more successful in two months by becoming really interested in other people's success than you can in two years trying to get other people interested in your own success"**
> **- Dale Carnegie**

8. Don't schmooze!

People can spot a schmoozer a million miles away: that person who is just trying to suck up to the biggest fish in the pond and will do or say anything to get there. What that schmoozer does not realize is that his own ambition is what is preventing him from ever making that connection, because he is being 100 percent selfish in his actions. He is the guy you are talking to and all the while his eyes wander around the room to see if there is someone more important to talk to. This behavior is rude and disrespectful. Period. Plus, it doesn't get you anywhere! Be 100 percent engaged in the conversation at hand (are you noticing a theme here?), and if you feel the need to move on then politely excuse yourself and thank the person for their time. Always make sure you are listening and not playing the numbers game that schmoozers play. You will win in the long run.

9. Network everywhere...like, everywhere!

People are people, right? Whether they are in your industry directly, indirectly, or they know someone in your industry... and people are everywhere! So anywhere you go and there is someone next to you in line, on the street corner, or at the table next to you in the coffee shop, your opportunity to get in the game never ends. Take advantage of the world and all the people in it!

Christine: I never thought this would happen, but we have met some of our best connections in show business at the playground. This was unintentional, believe us! I am usually in sweats, no makeup, and holding a cup of coffee like it's crack. But again, it's about building relationships, and when you take a genuine interest in someone else's pride and joy – their child – you bond naturally.

10. Be yourself, and have fun!

All of these tips and rules are here to help guide you, but ultimately you have to make networking work for you. If networking feels like net*working,* then you are doing something wrong. Networking and cultivating relationships is a process and a state of being, rather than an event. If it does not feel true to who you are, then don't do it. Make it a habit and be consistent. Whether you use a spreadsheet, your phone or sticky notes, continually update your relationship building and it will pay dividends.

It is true that if you want to succeed, you *must* make new connections, but *how* you do it is something you will have to navigate for yourself. We do not want you to get hung up on the word, "networking." Call it whatever you like, just remember, as long as you are being you, and broadcasting your "brand," you are "networking." If you are networking in the most genuine and human way possible, then everything else will flow from there. Just make sure there is more *fun* than work in the process and you will be thinking and networking like a Thriving Artist!

Now go make some new connections!

Chapter 6 – Focus On: Finances
Money Management and Asset Creation or
The Money Talk - Part 1

> *Disclaimer: We are not, nor have we ever claimed to be, financial professionals. Do not make any investment decisions without first consulting with a financial professional. We do not endorse the sale or purchase of any one or group of stocks, securities, mutual funds, or any financial product...etc. Everything we will talk about is what has worked for us, but that does not mean that it will work for you. You must do your own due diligence before making any financial decisions.*

With that disclaimer out of the way, let's now talk about one of our favorite topics: managing your money as an artist. So many emotions/thoughts/myths can come up when one thinks of the words "artist" and "money." If you have any residual fear or doubt about managing your money, that is fine, because we are going to cover that now and give you some tools to help you take control of your financial life.

> ## "The two most beautiful words in the English language are 'cheque enclosed.'"
> ### – Dorothy Parker

ASSET CREATION (YOUR INCOME-GENERATING SKILLS)
Wouldn't it be amazing to walk into an audition room and *not be emotionally attached to getting the job*? If you didn't have to worry about how you were going to pay your bills, wouldn't auditioning be a whole lot easier? You might be a lot more relaxed and probably have more fun in the process, right? You are also very likely to book more jobs! If you have ever sat behind the table during auditions (and we highly recommend you should) it is easy to see the people who are uptight, and they are *not* the ones who get the callback. The actors who are carefree, prepared, and have a great time in the room are the ones who get the

callback. If you are not financially desperate when you walk in the room, you are then completely free to do the work and not care about what happens when you walk out of the room.

So let's get the subject of "survival" taken care of right up front. It is our goal not to have you simply surviving, but to have you Thriving both on stage and off.

In this section we will talk about and outline some creative ways by which you can generate income that just may also further your career. Later in this section we will also cover different money management systems, as well as highlighting a specific set of skills in the area of personal finances.

While you already have artistic skills as an actor, singer, musician, painter, etc… you need to have other skills that generate income as well. What do we mean? Unless you are independently wealthy, or on the dole from a friend or relative, you are likely going to need income from other sources besides your art. Chances are, that you are eventually going to need a job: the "dreaded survival job," right? Wrong! Let's find a new way of thinking.

One of the things we always impart to anyone pursuing a life in the arts is to hone your non-artistic skills. Think about the other talents/skills you have apart from your artistic talent and ask yourself, "How can I make money from this skill?" For example: Are you great on the computer? Can you design websites? Can you proofread legal documents? Are you a bartender? Can you teach SAT prep or tutor? Can you teach dance, yoga, Pilates, music lessons…etc? Are you a great tour guide? Are you good at selling and talking to people? Can you type 90 words a minute? Are you a shutterbug who could start your own photography business? Can you launch your own jewelry line? These are just some of the skills that might be outside your artistic realm but will come in handy when it comes to making money. Not to be misunderstood, there is nothing wrong with waiting tables. We have both done it and it served us for a time. However, we are asking you to think outside the box.

Start by asking yourself the following: What are *you* great at? What can you do possibly better than anyone?

What skill do you have that you can turn into a consistent income stream?

Take a moment now and write down all your skills, then start brainstorming about how you can use those skills to your financial advantage. We recommend getting together with a few friends and doing this in a small group, because you may generate new ideas by sharing, or someone might tell you how great you are at something that you never thought of. You might be surprised at how much you can help other people, and how much other people can help you get your project(s) off the ground. Don't limit yourself here. If you can talk about something intelligently for 15 minutes or more, write it down.

Skills

Christine: I was watching TV the other night and saw a woman who had an idea that made her a mint. She loves to knit. She knits everywhere. She also liked going to the movies and she found it was hard to knit in a dark movie theatre. So she came up with the idea to attach a light to her knitting needles, and she has made herself a pretty penny with her idea. You can get lights on crocheting needles now too! She is a millionaire because she married a practical idea with something she was already good at and loved to do.

What could be your "million dollar" idea?

After you answer this question, ask yourself one more, specifically, "How can I create *leverage* with this idea/skill?" By that we mean, how can your idea make money while you sleep? What related products or services can you offer to people that they can purchase 24/7? Whom can you handpick to work with so you aren't doing everything yourself? Always keep these thoughts in mind because they will lead you to being a Thriving Artist, one with an ongoing income, rather than a starving one, only trading time for money. Get out of thinking that you have to work an hour to get paid for an hour! Get out of thinking that you have to do *all* the work on your business or project. There is no leverage in that way of thinking! There are only so many hours in the day and you only have so much energy. Always seek out a team and seek out leverage. Remember that you started this journey to thrive in your art, not to spend all your time on survival work! So really dig in, do some work, and *find out how you can creatively solve your income equation before there is ever a financial crisis staring you in the face.*

To kick-start your thinking we have a list below of some skills you may already have. Check all that apply to you and add others that we may have missed. *Then go put your skills to good financial use.* Take a chance on yourself! You just might create something you love that pays you more than you ever thought it could!

As we examine each of the examples below, we will (when possible) recommend products/services that we have access to that could amplify your efforts. Feel free to contact us for more information on any one of them and we will help you as much as possible.

Graphic/Web design	Mixologist/Bartender
Makeup artist	Transcriber/Type like a fiend
Proofreader	Drive a cab/Know your city
Babysitting/Working with children	Clean freak
Personal assistant/organizer	Workout maniac
Animal lover	Photographer
Accounting	Smarty pants
Playing an instrument/Choral/Singing	Construction/Handyman
Nutritional consultant/Personal chef	
Your ideas here . . .	

Now, let's break down each one of these skills and point out some jobs that will pay the bills so you don't have to ask, "Do you want fries with that?" For all of these examples, we can name at least two people who have worked or are currently working in these fields to happily make ends meet.

GRAPHIC/WEB DESIGN

1. Build websites for businesses or fellow actors and/or create graphic designs for logos, page artwork, etc.

2. Work for a big corporation in their graphic design.

Joe: I partnered with a top web development company and work as a partner, referring business to the team of designers and technicians. I don't have to know anything about HTML or any other coding language and still get to work in a very lucrative market on a part-time basis. Contact us via our website www.TheThrivingArtists.com/contactus.html if you have interests or talent in website development and would like to have a discussion about this way of generating income. To check out the company I work with, just go to www.ThrivingWebSolutions.com

MIXOLOGIST/BARTENDER

1. If you have great bartending skills, seek out a job with a company that offers benefits and work to arrange your schedule so you will not have to close the bar at 4 a.m.

2. Get creative and think up new drinks/concoctions that you can pitch to bars/restaurants.

3. Start your own company and *only* work at private parties. Have a theme or a gimmick that sets you apart from everyone else. Do you flip bottles? Can you change the theme of your bar at any time? Perhaps you can have a website that sells a deck of cards with your unique drink recipes on it? You just have to come up with 52 of them!

MAKEUP ARTIST

1. If you love makeup and are experienced with technique, partner with a head-shot photographer and get paid $100 to $150 (or more) per session for your services.

2. Work on film/TV sets.

3. Do bridal parties/bachelorette parties/girls night out; if you think this last one is crazy, think again. There are a lot of people who have money and will gladly spend it to look good for a special night out.

4. Use and sell your own makeup line!

Christine: I have been doing this successfully for several years now, so when the bride, actor, or corporate type loves what I put on them, I can just reach into my kit and sell it to them on the spot! Or better yet, I set an appointment to customize their makeup to match their skin tone exactly. I have a client for life because she can't get that blend anywhere but through me! Also because of my makeup skills, I save myself quite a bit of cash when it comes time to take my headshots! To learn more email Christine at info@TheThrivingArtists.com

TRANSCRIBER/TYPE LIKE A FIEND

1. Work as an executive assistant and earn $15 to $20 dollars (or more) per hour because you can accurately type 90 words a minute.

2. Make your own hours by transcribing either for a company or at home.

Joe: I was on a bus and truck tour of Funny Girl and one of my cast mates did this the whole time we were on the road. She would get the recordings sent to her and then would be typing away as we rode the bus rather than watching movies. She made money while she was making money... not a bad idea, right? There are tons of ways to monetize all of those little pockets of time that could otherwise be lost to boredom or the latest YouTube video. You just have to seek them out!

PROOFREADER

1. There are big bucks in this if you are good at it. You can make your own hours and/or work from home (are you catching a theme here?)

2. Specialize in legal documents and work for legal firms that will offer you health benefits. Perhaps if you work late at night at the office, they may give you a free car service to take you home... hey, it beats a crazy cab ride! That is, if crazy cab rides aren't your thing.

3. Check out www.PaidToProofread.com for more information and to reach out to our friend Sue Gilad, who got paid to read The DaVinci Code!

DRIVE A CAB/KNOW THE CITY

1. You are a great driver and happen to know the quickest route to the airport at rush hour. (If you already are a cab driver, please disregard that "crazy cab ride" comment in the previous paragraph.)

2. Be a tour guide either with Big Apple Tours, Star Tours, or any company catering to tourists.

3. Conduct walking tours of your favorite areas of the city.

4. Start your own company and customize your tours depending on your groups and how vigorously they would like to walk. Take people to see specific "artist haunts" that no other touring company would know about!

BABYSITTING/WORKING WITH CHILDREN

1. Babysitting/nannying: the epitome of making your own hours. Try to find fellow artists with children. You will mostly be working at night and your days will be free for classes and auditions!

2. Become a "child guardian" for a Broadway show. Any show on Broadway that has children in it must have a certain number of guardians per number of children in the show. This is a great opportunity to see the industry from a completely different perspective. Our good friend Amanda worked with the younger cast members of Billy Elliot for several years and developed a love for teaching. She is now a "teaching artist" and is blossoming into another great career!

3. Work/perform at children's birthday parties: there are many opportunities here. There are existing companies you can work with or start your own.

4. Teach dance/voice/painting/instrumental lessons to children. There are plenty of parents out there who are happy to give their children a few extra lessons per week… why not pay you to do it?

Joe: While I was out on the national tour of Shrek the Musical I taught one of the girls who played Young Fiona tap, jazz, and ballet lessons anywhere from one to three times a week. We had a great time and she was happy to continue training even though she was out on the road away from her home studio. I was happy to keep my teaching skills sharp and to come up with new ways to teach and keep things interesting for her. It was a win-win for sure.

CLEAN FREAK

1. Clean apartments/homes. For some people this is very therapeutic; put on your headphones and go to town!

2. Clean yoga/dance studios in exchange for classes at a work-study rate.

Joe: I did this when I was first in NYC at Broadway Dance Center and loved it! No, I didn't love the cleaning, but it was an easy way to keep my cost for classes way down. I was taking class nearly every day of the week and saved a ton of money with the work-study program.

PERSONAL ASSISTANT/ORGANIZER

1. Be a personal assistant, organizing people's homes, offices. You can certainly make your own hours and charge what you are worth.

2. Teach people how to better manage and organize their time/lives.

3. Be a personal assistant to a star or high-powered executive who needs someone to help out with things they don't have time to do. In Los Angeles, this is a very popular side job and can be very eye-opening and exciting.

Christine: I am pretty good at organizing, specifically financial stuff. I can do wonders with your receipts, filing cabinets, music, scripts, etc. I was working for a friend in this capacity and she recommended me to a few other people. At one point, I was working for three different people. I could make my own hours and I wasn't missing auditions or working until late at night. PS – we are going to need a personal assistant very soon. So if you live in LA and are interested, look us up!

WORKOUT MANIAC

1. Be a personal trainer, yoga, or Pilates instructor. You get to make your own hours and stay fit in the process. You can do this at a gym, by going to people's homes or both.

2. Dance teacher/fitness coach. Lots of gyms are offering classes that are both dance and workout oriented. Why not look at your personal skills and create a class that is unique to you? What special flare can you give your class/workout? You just might find yourself with a nice following from class to class! Somebody very clever created Zumba and it's now a huge hit in gyms across the country.

3. Offer a line of vitamin supplements to your private clients. You have trust and relationship built in and they are already more likely to listen to you than to anyone else about what they should take. There are lots of lines out there, so do your homework on them before you would represent any specific company.

Contact us at www.TheThrivingArtists.com/contactus.html for specific product recommendations.

ANIMAL LOVER

1. Be a dog walker, either with a company or on your own.

2. Take care of people's pets/apartment while they are away on vacation.

3. Offer products related to pet care… there is money to be made! Some people treat their pets better than they treat themselves or their families. We had a wonderful Scottish terrier named Emmy and we used a terrific product that kept her healthy as could be until she was fourteen and a half years old (ancient for a Scottie).

PHOTOGRAPHER

1. If this is a passion of yours and you have talent or interest in this area, be the photographer at friend's weddings/anniversaries/birthdays, etc. The word will get out and you will get work.

2. If you are serious about being a photographer, get yourself a website!

3. We both know many people who started taking headshots for friends and it has turned into quite a secondary and sometimes primary source of income for them. A few Thriving Artist photographers that we would like to mention here are:

> Kim Carson www.KimCarsonPhotography.com
> Stacey Turner www.lemonsqueezystudio.com
> Brad Roller www.BradRollerPhotography.com

They all have thriving careers and businesses at the same time!

ACCOUNTING

1. Start doing your friends'/coworkers' taxes.

2. Help friends/coworkers with their finances/budget planning.

SMARTY PANTS

Ok, admit it: You are a bookworm. That's great! Now make that interest pay you.

1. Tutor, either as a general tutor or a specific subject, and become *the* person to study with!

2. Teach SAT/ACT/GMAT preparation.

3. Be a substitute teacher if you have the proper degree.

PLAYING INSTRUMENTS/CHORAL/SINGING

1. Teach instrumental lessons.

2. Teach voice/sight singing/ear training lessons.

3. Coach singers for auditions.

4. Transpose music/play music to be recorded for practicing.

Joe and Christine: Our friend, Warren Freeman, started a fantastic business in which he does audition coaching and fast music recording for auditions. When someone has a callback and gets music to learn all they have to do is email it to Warren, he plays it and creates a digital file, then emails it back to you. No more scrambling to find someone to meet with when there is no time left in the day. Check him out at www.GetOnMySides.com. You will be glad you did!

5. Do church jobs as a singer or musician.

6. Jingle singing.

7. Get in (or start) a band and gig around town at weddings/events.

NUTRITIONAL CONSULTANT/PERSONAL CHEF

1. Personally coach people on their diets and how to eat more healthfully.

2. Customize recipes and meal plans for your clients. Do you have a specialty dish? Are you vegetarian or vegan and know a lot of great recipes?

3. Can you create a cookbook for actors while they are on tour and only have hotpots, microwaves and fridges? Anything is possible right?

CONSTRUCTION/HANDYMAN
1. Do cosmetic construction work on people's homes.

2. Patch walls, paint rooms, install new cabinets, put in/refinish a new hardwood floor, stain or refurbish older furniture, etc.

3. Paint custom murals on the walls. Come up with ideas for baby nurseries, play/ game rooms, garages, etc.

4. *When you clean up* (like every good handyman does) possibly offer cleaning product(s) or your favorite tools to sell as an additional moneymaker for you.

Do any of these income-generating ideas sound appealing? Of course these are not the only ones out there, and if you are currently waiting tables, slinging drinks, or answering phones and you love doing it, then by all means continue to do so. We simply wanted to open up your thinking to new and creative ways of generating income while you grow your career. Do some digging and see what you can come up with on your own!

After you figure out how you want to get paid when you aren't working at your art, our best advice would be to *go get started*! Do it now. Choose your skill, choose your team that will help you, and then go *do it*! Fake it until you make it. We love the motto; Ready, Fire, Aim! You don't have to know exactly how it is going to unfold, but taking bold action will lead you to the people and resources you need to make it a reality. Do. It. Now.

Below are a few examples of artists who are creatively generating income. They are either currently in a show, just finished a show, or going to do a show.

Example #1
We will begin with Matthew LaBanca. Matt was in the original cast of the Broadway show *Young Frankenstein*. Some of you may remember when Roger Bart injured his back and had to miss nine performances; Matt took over for those performances as Dr. Fredrick Frankenstein. He has never had to wait tables or

answer phones and he owns his apartment. Matt is also looking into purchasing more real estate and expanding his investment portfolio. He will share with you how he used his various skills to make money and has never had to hold down a typical "survival job."

We asked the bolded questions, with Matt's responses directly below each question.

How long have you lived in New York?
I've lived in NY (on and off) since June 2000. Since then, I've traveled all over with theatre jobs, sometimes for months at a time, but I've always kept an apartment here.

What did you do for money when you first moved here?
I started booking out-of-town theatre jobs. During that first year, I stayed in NY for only four to five months altogether. I went where the work was – at the time, working in a show was more important to me than staying here. I'd also had a good amount of savings. For the first two years after graduating from UConn, I was touring with shows, and I was able to save a lot of that money because I had no student loans or credit card debt. Starting out with that cushion helped my mindset *a lot*, even if I didn't really live off of it.

What skills other than acting, singing and dancing can you utilize to make ends meet?
I have a degree in music education, so I can teach (in schools or out of my apartment). I play a few instruments and have used those skills for income.

What jobs have you had during your tenure so far?
My "go-to" job has always been church work. I've been a church singer/musician for years, all through high school and college, and again here in NYC. It's a good fit, because the weekend masses allow for flexibility with auditions, plus I feel like I'm part of a community. Weddings and funerals often come my way. The work pays very well for the time commitment.

Would you do anything differently?
Probably not, I'm glad I stuck to my guns!

Do you believe in living off your savings while waiting for the next job to come around?

I don't really like to do that. I think it's important to maintain a cushion of money around you, especially as a performing artist. If you have the ability to work, then work! There may be some point where you get injured and cannot work, even at a survival job – that's happened to several people I know, and it's scary. If you've eaten into or depleted your savings, then what do you do? Some people I know have had to move back to their parents' houses in their thirties – that really stinks.

Being an actor doesn't automatically mean being a "bohemian" actor. I want a good, solid lifestyle. Planning for retirement, a second home, investments, my baby fund, (I want to start a family sometime in the next five to ten years): they all take money. I'd rather use my savings for things like that, instead of my daily living expenses.

What advice could you give other artists on how to live in New York powerfully?

You have to have a balance between your head and your heart. I think a big key to maintaining life as an actor or an artist is the flexibility in the financial area of your life. If you can be creative enough to have different sources of income coming your way, it settles your mind so that your creative spark can thrive.

I also think it makes a big difference if you do something every day to keep in touch with your art, no matter how small. Doing that brings joy into your life, and keeps yourself focused on why you came to NY to begin with.

Awesome, right? Matt is successful both as an artist and in his financial life, because he understood at an early age that making money creatively and with talents he already possesses could be fun and makes his life a lot easier. He auditions when he wants, can coach and train at his leisure, and can position himself to land the job of a lifetime!

For more information about Matt and his upcoming projects check out www.MatthewLabanca.com

Make sure that you share your Thriving Artists stories. We want to hear how your fabulous skill(s) have given you the financial freedom and time to pursue your dream! Send your story to info@TheThrivingArtists.com

---

THE ECONOMIC LANDSCAPE OF SHOW BUSINESS

So you have the money thing solved…brilliant. You are really enjoying the job that pays the bills, and your outlook on life is far better than if you were doing some "soul-sucking" work just to make a buck. You are walking the path of a Thriving Artist! Congratulations!

Now that you aren't stressed about paying the rent, and what you do to pay the rent makes you happy, let's take a moment and examine the economic landscape of *show business.*

Note: here we will speak directly from our experiences and knowledge of our art form (acting), however the themes are universal and apply to any and every career path as an artist.

What we are going to break down next is the different ways we, as artists, earn our income. The breakdown is in four categories. Keeping with the theme of acting and show business, we will call them "Actors," "Stars/Specialties," "Creators/Writers," and "Producers/Investors." In all of the following, remember that no one way is right or wrong. You simply are where you are. If you want to make a change, this information will be very helpful in identifying your "here" so you can eventually get to "there." As artists, we are very lucky in that we have the ability to use our creativity to make beautiful art while getting paid for doing it. Some artists cross into more than one category, and now you will see how it might be possible for you to do this as well. Let's take a look now at the different ways one generates income in "the business," along with the pros and cons of each.

ACTORS

We as actors (in a musical or play), being zany, wacky, wonderful, wild, and creative, are, at the end of the day, *employees.* We work for someone else and get paid for it. We are worker bees and we earn a wage. Usually we see a paycheck once a week, and it is for roughly the same amount. We love what we do, and 99 percent of the time, coming to work is a joyous realization of a dream we had from the time we were kids. Artistically speaking, when you are working, life is great! From a financial standpoint it's great too, however, if we don't come to work for whatever reason, we don't get paid. That is the textbook definition of employee. You show up at work, do your job, and get paid a steady wage or salary for it. There is nothing wrong with being a worker bee, especially if you love your work. Many people like to come to work six days a week and to know they'll have a steady paycheck.

The key is to understand what the financial limitations are of being an Actor. If you need to make more money or you are sick of working for someone else, then just being in the Actor category may not be ideal for making your financial dreams come true. However, being an Actor in a longer-running show does give you the opportunity to learn to manage your finances on a different level, as you now have money coming in steadily each week. We will explore the topic of money management in more depth later, but for now we will stick with how the money is generated. Most of us know that a *steady* paycheck as an Actor is almost a paradox. Nonetheless it is a valid way of making money as an artist and one that appeals to thousands upon thousands of people.

So what are the pros and cons to being an Actor in a show?

Let's start with some pros:

1. You are doing what you love more than anything in the world and getting paid for it. What a wonderful thing to be able to say!

2. A paycheck. Practically everyone loves a weekly paycheck. (People who say money isn't important are either lying or broke). With a steady income you can pay off debt if you have it, you can save up and buy that new tech gadget you've been longing for, or you can just save a boatload of money! You are not praying every night that the federal government keeps extending the unemployment benefits. A feeling of stability is no longer a wish…it is a reality.

3. Security. This applies to long-running shows or tours, and it sure is nice when it happens.

4. Payment into your 401(k) and pension. This is something that often goes overlooked. Every time Actors do an Equity show, the producers are paying money into our pension and health funds. We are building our retirement fund and some Actors aren't even aware of it. Have you ever really looked at that statement that comes from Equity once a year? It illustrates that you will make X amount a month once you retire. We love looking at our statements because, as we will teach you, they are part of your financial picture that you need to keep track

of on an ongoing basis. As for your 401(k), in some contracts (e.g., Broadway, most Equity touring contracts) the producer automatically contributes (usually 3 percent) into your fund every week. If you are also contributing part of your gross weekly salary, you are saving even more money *and* lowering your taxable income. A win/win situation for sure! (Note: You must pay attention to the markets that your 401(k) is invested in. More on that later.)

5. Earning health insurance weeks. As of this writing we need twelve weeks of Equity work for six months of health coverage, and twenty weeks of Equity work for a full year of coverage. (There is a "look back" system that Equity has set up as to when your insurance will kick in, but in simple terms, it will start at the beginning of the next quarter after you qualify.)

Now some cons:

1. Salary is limited (to a degree). If you are in the ensemble of a show, your salary will generally coincide with what the Equity minimum is for that contract. Yes, you have your extras like understudy pay, hazard pay, and so on, which will bump you up a bit, but you will still be in the ballpark of the minimum. If you are a lead, you usually have some leeway to negotiate here, especially with some nice credits behind you.

Some of you may say minimum pay on whatever contract you are working is fine with you. When Christine booked her first production contract in 2001, the going salary was fine with her too! As time goes on, however, things change.

Sometimes salaries or per diem only go up $8 to $10 per week every six months or a year. The price of food, gas, and the basic cost of living can certainly skyrocket faster than that.

For an example, say you are in a long-running Broadway show. You are able to cover all of your expenses (rent and bills) with about two to two and a half weeks worth of your salary. So you are roughly saving one and a half to two weeks of your salary per month. But remember, this is before you see a movie, make an impulse purchase, or take a trip somewhere. At this point, unless something changes in your routine that is the set amount of money you have to work with month after month. You will get pay bumps when you go on for your understudy part and when the Equity minimum goes up; otherwise, it is somewhat like being retired and living on a fixed income, only here you are doing eight shows a week for that fixed income!

But for the sake of argument, let's say that you create and stick to a budget. All of a sudden, you get in a car accident and it's going to cost you $1,000 to fix your car and your insurance premium is going up. Luckily, you have saved some money, so you are covered. A few months go by and you need a new air conditioner in your apartment. *Please note: We are not trying to be "doom and gloom" on you. Ask anyone: Life happens and expenses come up, usually when we least expect them.* So while a long-running Broadway show is *amazing*, you are always going to make a fixed amount of money, because you are a worker bee and worker bees only get so much per week no matter what.

2. Time constraints. Yes, a steady gig is great and we all love them, but eight shows a week can take a toll on your offstage life after a while. Joe was fortunate to work many years in a row on tour and then Broadway, but he did miss some "life" stuff. Did he want to? No, of course not, but that's the nature of working six days a week. You might miss your cousin's wedding, your class reunion, or a lot of out-of-town birthdays. If you have children who are in school or on sports teams, you may miss a lot of activities/events they are in, such as baseball games or school plays. None of this is a complaint, it's just a reality, and for some people, this can be harder to bear as time goes on.

3. Feeling like you have to stay in a show. This can happen when you increase your standard of living to a point where the weekly check goes from being a luxury to a necessity. Life can get expensive! It could be that you are the main income generator of the family, or your spouse recently lost his/her job. When things like this happen you may have to stay in a job/show that you feel you have outgrown. A recent survey found that 55 percent of Americans are in jobs they either don't like or would like to change. We hope that's not the case when you are in your long-running Broadway show! Unfortunately though, we have all sat down and watched a Broadway show and been hugely disappointed when an actor on stage is apparently "phoning it in." They should just quit, right? We think so too, but maybe financially they can't. Certainly that is *no excuse* for giving a lazy performance, but it happens. We have both known many people who are doing a show solely for the paycheck and not because they want to do the

show or role anymore. They have debt or bills that need to be paid, college tuition for their kids…the list goes on and on. Feeling trapped in a show hinges on your approach and outlook toward the work you are doing, and is therefore something you can control but we felt it warranted mentioning, as it is a very common trap that people fall into while being artistic worker bees.

STARS/SPECIALTY PERFORMERS

People who are "Stars/Specialty Performers" are:

Solo cabaret performers

People with one-man/one-woman shows

People who write a full show and star in it every time it is mounted

People who are a headline act on a concert tour

Stand up comics

Street performers

Clowns

Mimes

Stars/Specialty Performers are the ones who are responsible for creating, booking, and managing all of their work. They operate outside the realm of a salaried actor in a show, who gets a steady paycheck every week. For these Star/Specialty artists to get paid, they have to drum up and book their work, or have a team to do it for them. The main difference between being an Actor and being a Star/Specialty is that while the actor typically makes a *wage*, which never changes, the Star/Specialty makes a *profit* depending on the price he/she can command for their work. Wages are limited, while profits can be limit*less*. If they are booked steadily with high-paying gigs, then profits go up. There is generally no set rate that a Star/Specialty will make unless it is one they have set for themselves, which is known as a "quote." A stand-up comic may make $20,000 in one night working at a big casino in Las Vegas and then $2,000 the next night in a smaller town if he is willing to take the work there. It is all up to the performer and the rate can fluctuate. Of course the opposite is true as well…if you're not booked, you're not making any money.

The main similarity that both of these examples share is this: if you don't show up, you don't get paid. As an Actor in a show, this is common sense. If you miss a show you get docked a portion of your salary. If you are a Star/Specialty who created your work and are the only one who performs it, it is obvious that if *you* aren't there, you won't get paid.

All of this is to impress the point that as an Actor or a Star/Specialty there is a *finite* amount of money you can make because there is only a finite amount of time you can devote to your craft in a day. In the landscape of show business we just want to create an awareness of where you are. It's not a good or bad thing; it is simply perspective on how you might generate income through your art.

Let's take a quick look at the pros and cons of being a Star/Specialty.

Some pros:

1. No boss, just you. Having no one to answer to can be priceless and, to some, the ultimate definition of freedom. We know a lot of artists who were just never satisfied doing the work of others. It was nice for the paycheck, but in the end it left them wanting more. In the case of being a Star/Specialty, there is no creative team who can fire you, and generally nobody you have to answer to. You are free to hand-pick your material and your dream team to help fulfill *your* artistic vision. In the end, all decisions rest on your shoulders. Some artists love that responsibility and if you are one of them, perhaps being a Star/Specialty is for you. Write your own cabaret act or one-person show and make it happen!

2. Make your own hours and schedule. Going along with being your own boss, this is a major perk to your "real life" schedule.

Christine: I already mentioned that I did the tour of The Best Little Whorehouse in Texas *starring Ann-Margret. Years later she was doing her revue show in Atlantic City and my family and I went to see her. Aside from it being a fantastic show and a wonderful reunion, we had a conversation about her life post-*Whorehouse. *Because the cabaret was her show and she called the shots, there were no shows booked over the holidays! She wanted to be with her family and felt that her fellow cast and crew should do the same. This is the type of fabulous control you can have when you are in this position.*

3. You can choose what markets to play. For instance, if you have a great solo act and you want to see the world, you can set yourself up as a long-term guest entertainer on a cruise line, or you can hop from ship to ship on different lines.

The world, quite literally, is your oyster. Work from home or close to home, or in a certain region. You have the complete freedom to choose where you will accept work. If you are a performer in a traveling show (like we were with *Shrek the Musical* as we wrote this) you have no say in the booking. We perform wherever the tour is booked, for better or for worse. Being a Star/Specialty, you get to choose where you go and when, which can be a lovely thing indeed.

4. You set your price. You determine what you will get paid, and you never have to settle for less than you think you are worth. Whatever product you are putting out there, you are now playing the game of supply and demand, and if you are in demand, then the sky is the limit for you!

Joe: I was working as a guest entertainer on a cruise line in early 2010 and crossed paths with a solo musician who was also a guest entertainer on ships, and had been for some time. He was in his mid-twenties, had a great act in which he played saxophone, sang, and told a few stories in about a forty-five- to fifty-minute set. He was having the time of his life and got to name his price because he was in demand. Guest entertainers are generally on the ship around eight days, and in that time they will usually perform two nights doing two shows each night. The rest of the time was just a paid vacation. If that sounds like a lifestyle you want, definitely look into that venue!

Some cons:

1. Taking a risk. Whenever you create your own act, you are taking a much bigger risk. There is no guarantee that the act you are creating will be commercially successful. Some people argue that commercial success with your art is "selling out" or somehow compromising yourself. We don't feel that way at all. As long as you stay true to who you are and do what you love, we believe that success (also known as money) is bound to come your way. We are not going to get into the "art for art's sake" conversation. The simple point is this: If you choose to do your own thing artistically, you are taking on the risk of it not generating enough income to make ends meet if your show doesn't sell. That's just the way it is and you have to decide if that is the career path you want to take. It is risky, but the rewards are equally as great.

2. You have to create your "system" from scratch. What do we mean by that? Your invoices for payment, your logo, your bookings, the way your business model is

set up, finding your makeup artists/hair people and paying them, etc. Now some of those things can be very creative and perhaps even fun. Some people find creating a logo or choosing a team for their show challenging and stimulating, and others perhaps not. Either way, you don't have co-workers to offload responsibility on, or a boss you can go to for advice, at least not right away. Again, it's completely up to you who you will surround yourself with in your business.

3. Hand-picking your team can be a blessing and a curse. If you need to hire people, it is obviously a sign that your show and booking rate is growing and you are doing great. Congratulations! However, we all know that the same people who make our lives easier can also create complications. For example, they may show up late, complain, underperform, and/or get sick/leave town/quit when you are swamped. Unless you find extremely dedicated people, there is likely to be some sort of personnel turnover or management issues and it can lead to a lot of headaches.

Now, you may look at these cons and think to yourself, "No way am I doing that!" The statistics alone can be staggering (but you would not be reading this book if you were worried about the odds, now would you?). Some people disagree and believe that the risks are outweighed by the rewards of creating life and art on their own terms. There is also the wage versus profit argument. You have to ask yourself whether you are willing to walk an even thinner edge in doing your own work, and making the (sometimes inconsistent yet potentially huge) profit from that, or would you rather bring the work of others to life and get paid on a weekly basis? There is no right or wrong answer, just the one that is right for you. While you are taking a risk to be a Star/Specialty, once you are successful, there is no limit to how much profit you can make. Ultimately, it is up to you to decide how you will find the balance of being artistically fulfilled and at that same time financially sound.

Of course, there is always the option of creating your Star/Specialty show while in your steady paycheck gig as an Actor. We know many people, ourselves included, who got some of our best work done on other projects while performing in a long-running show. This is especially true if you are on the road. Now that is the Thriving Artist way indeed!

CREATOR/WRITER

An example of a Creator/Writer would be:

Composer

Lyricist

Writer

Director

Choreographer

Designer

These artists do not audition for shows like Actors do, because they help *create* the show from the ground up. These folks write the music, direct, choreograph, design the costumes & sets, etc.

The main thing that distinguishes the Creator/Writer group from the Actors and Star/Specialty performers is that these people create their work, see it fully produced, and most often *get paid for it each and every time it is used.*

As an example, let's suppose that a choreographer is hired by a producer to choreograph a new show. During the entire time that the show is in rehearsals and previews, that choreographer is like an Actor, meaning he will get paid a weekly salary (or possibly a set fee to choreograph the show). The compensation arrangement changes once the show opens. The choreographer now gets a weekly residual or "royalty" that was negotiated up front, *and he makes that money every week the show is open.*

The exciting point to note here is that his work is done and he's still getting paid! Who among us would like to go to bed at night, and then wake up in the morning with more money in the bank? Let's take a look at what is possible. Let's say, for example, the choreographer is earning $5,000 per week in royalties. This choreographer is now *earning money* while sitting at home doing nothing or possibly already working on another project and making an income from that. This is called passive or residual income that is being generated by something called an "asset."

To know if something is an "asset," you only need to answer one question: Every week, does it put money into your pocket, or does it take money out of your pocket? "Assets" put money *in your pocket* while "liabilities" take money out of your pocket. Assets are a very nice thing! How would you like to earn $5,000 per week *while* you are looking for your next creative project?

Now let us assume that the choreographer's show is a big hit, and they are opening two national tours, as well as shows in London, Australia, and a European tour. That's five more productions running simultaneously with the Broadway production, and our choreographer will get $5,000 per week for every production that his/her work is used. That's an additional $25,000 more every week, for a total of $30,000 a week for as long as all of those productions run. So hypothetically in a year, our choreographer will have a gross profit of $1.56 million! And here is the greatest thing of all: He/she did the creative work only *once*! That seems a little better than being a steady wage earner, right? Herein lies the huge difference between creating art that pays you a profit, and just being the person in the art making a wage.

(The numbers indicated here are purely used as an example.)

The same sort of royalty situation applies, though the amounts vary greatly, to everyone on the creative side who builds the show from scratch: composer, lyricist, director, and choreographer. Every time that show is mounted, those people get paid. Of course, there is no reward without risk so let's look that the ups and downs of being a Creator/Writer.

Some pros:

1. Once again, you are creating your own art. How fabulous is that? How many times have we auditioned for parts that of course we could do, but may not be the perfect fit. When you create a show, you can write yourself the perfect part!

2. Possible double-dipping. You can get paid as both an Actor and Creator/ Writer of your new hit show! Harvey Fierstein has done this a few times. In the musical *A Catered Affair* he was both an Actor and a Writer, collecting two paychecks.

3. Duplication and leverage. If your show gets picked up at multiple theatres, you can really earn a substantial profit. This is the major difference between being a Star/Specialty and a Creator/Writer. The Star/Specialties don't generally make money in their sleep. They could if they duplicated their show and had other people play their part, but Creator/Writers, by the nature of what they do, already

have their work duplicated. They don't have to be there at every performance in order to get paid.

Cons:

1. The cons of being a Creator/Writer are similar to those of a Star/Specialty (see above). There is a lot of risk to being a Creator/Writer for sure. There is no guarantee that anyone will ever buy into or invest in your work, or possibly commission you to create something for them. That is just part of the territory; there is little to no safety net at all when you are in this group. The rewards are equal to the risk, and the risk is substantial.

2. It costs a lot of money to get a project off the ground. If you are independently wealthy and can fund everything yourself, that is fantastic. Most Creator/Writers have to rely on the money of others for their projects to ever see the light of day.

3. Time and effort…lots of it. The current trend for a show to be born and then fully produced at the Broadway level can take anywhere from five to ten years. Jonathan Larson started working on *RENT* back in 1989 and it debuted off-Broadway on January 25, 1996. (Joe also recently spoke with the director of the film *The Impossible* starring Ewan McGregor, and learned it took him four and a half years from conception to completed film.)

Joe: I was on the first national tour of Hairspray *and we were playing Boston in October of 2003. A few miles up the road at North Shore Music Theatre a little show called* Memphis *was having its world debut production. I had a friend in the cast so I went to see it on our day off. I absolutely loved it and learned from the cast that the creative team had aspirations of bringing their show to Broadway. Six years later, on October 19, 2009 that dream came true, along with several Tony® Awards, including Best New Musical for the 2010 season. Anything can happen; it's just a matter of time and dedication to your dream!*

Before going on, let's look at the three groups we have covered so far:

Actors: Performers in a show, stagehands, stage managers. All fall into this group because if they don't show up for work, they don't make any money. There is no leverage and no residual income generated. They work for a relatively fixed wage, even if the show is making huge amounts of money at the box office.

Star/Specialty: Shows or artistic events that are created by or for one person. This group is made up of painters, sculptors, solo concert musicians (vocal or instrumental), cabaret performers, etc.

These artists get paid based on the demand for their work and earn a profit rather than any sort of steady income or wage on a weekly basis. Their income is *dependent* on supply and demand; in other words, *only* the artist can supply the art and will get paid only if there is a demand for that art. If the artist is a concert vocalist and sells out Madison Square Garden he/she stands to make a lot more money that night than if he/she sells out a ninety-nine-seat black box theatre.

These artists take a higher risk and should the market demand their talent, they stand to make a much higher profit.

Creators/Writers: Here is where a dramatic shift occurs. Once the show is mounted, the play is written, the music composed, the steps are choreographed, etc., this artist's work is essentially done. They no longer have to be present for that work to generate income, and every time the show/play/film is performed anywhere in the world, the Creator/Writer gets paid. In the case of a Broadway show, the creative team will frequently check in and have clean-up rehearsals to maintain the quality of their work. So, yes, they are still "working" on the piece, but largely they are removed from the process and are free to work on new projects. When we look at a film, the same rules apply with how the Creator/Writer artists are paid. However, film distribution is usually global and therefore profits can be considerably higher in the short term, especially if the film gets a wide distribution and is well received.

Other artists who are not necessarily Creators/Writers but who still can receive residual payment are those who do voice-over campaigns or take part in the early workshops of a new Broadway-bound musical. These artists are like an offshoot of the Creator/Writer group, but are worth mentioning here as we are examining the idea of generating residual or ongoing income. We will cover the idea of taking a Thriving Artists approach and belonging to several groups in just a bit. For now we have one more group left to examine.

PRODUCERS/INVESTORS

They do exactly what their group title says: produce and invest in shows, films, artists, musicians, etc. They gather all of the resources necessary to create a successful production. However, the two are not one and the same, so a distinction needs to be made between them.

In brief, an Investor is a person, group of people, or corporation(s) who pool their money together and put it toward the startup costs of a show. Investors are typically the "money people" and they have little, if any, artistic say in how the project develops. The amount of input is always directly proportional to the amount of money they have invested. More money equals more input.

Producers, on the other hand, are people who have to wear several hats and are the "hand shakers and deal makers." They facilitate the process of assembling the artistic team, while at the same time speaking to investors to make sure all the capital is in place so everything is paid for. A lead producer will also have a large amount of artistic input on the project/show as it develops and can often have a final say in anything from design choices to casting decisions. Producers may also put some of their own money into a show.

From an income standpoint, Producers/Investors are somewhat like Creators/ Writers, because they get paid from the profit of a show, which has limitless potential, as opposed to a fixed weekly wage (i.e., the compensation for the Actors). Producers (not Investors) may also receive a fee on the front end for their services in assembling the creative team, maintaining a production office with support staff, and finding all the investors to finance the project. After the show is running, the Producer/Investor's bottom line is determined by the net profit of the show (weekly box office income minus the operating costs).

Let us go back to the hit show example, which has five companies running worldwide, each of them bringing in approximately $1.1 million weekly. Here is the math: The show has a fixed weekly running cost of $500,000, which means the remaining $600,000 is pure profit to be divided up among the creative team, producers, and investors. Not too shabby, right? Now let's have fun and just say you had a 3 percent stake in the show. That comes out to $18,000 per week (3 percent of $600,000). Every week the show runs, at that profit level, that's what you take home. If every one of the five companies around the world generated the same business, that would make your income $90,000 per week, or $4.68 million per year. Think you could squeak by on that? Oh, and remember the fun part: All you did was Produce and/or Invest. You do not have to get up and go to work eight shows a week in order to get paid.

Of course, these numbers are simply for example, and the real process of how Producers/Investors get paid is a bit more complicated because there are more factors in the equation, but at its core, this is what happens.

When you think of Producers or Investors in a Broadway show, you might be thinking of people like Oprah Winfrey (*The Color Purple*), Disney (*The Lion King, Beauty and the Beast, The Little Mermaid, Mary Poppins*), Richard Frankel Productions (*Hairspray, The Producers, Sweeney Todd, Young Frankenstein, Gypsy*...among many others), or perhaps DreamWorks (*Shrek the Musical*). These are people who seem way out of our league. They are worth hundreds of millions of dollars, so investing in a show they are passionate about is probably nothing, right? How could this ever be a serious artistic venture for me, who doesn't have that kind of money (yet!)?

Guess what? There are plenty of people who Produce/Invest who didn't have money when they started either. What some Actors are now doing is getting together with other Actors and forming an LLC (or some business entity) in order to expand into this realm of show business. For example, five people form Production Company LLC and each contributes $1,000. They take that $5,000 and go in to purchase a small "unit" of a show that is raising money. Once the show is up and running, the group they formed will be paid any profit that is made and it will then be dispersed among the group. We have several friends who are currently invested in shows running on Broadway, and at the same time are still performing on Broadway or elsewhere. Once again, it is a two-paycheck game; one paycheck is from their active participation in going to work every day, and the other is from a one-time investment that could pay them on an ongoing basis.

So why would you invest in a Broadway show? We know there are tons of other investment opportunities out there that are *far* less risky. The majority of shows produced on Broadway never make a profit. Shows are considered "hits" simply because they make back their initial investment. But, if Broadway is where your

Producing/Investing heart lies, then do your research, connect with the right people, and do your best to choose/create a winner!

Also, Producing/Investing does not only have to be for Broadway. There are lots of new works out there that have a long life in regional theaters before making their Broadway debut. Some stay very active in the regional circuit and have a very long and profitable life there. There are also the realms of television, film, music groups, artists, etc. that we have barely mentioned here. The main thing to understand is that if you feel passionately about a person or project and want them to get seen, and you have some extra cash or could raise the money, then go for it! Nothing is stopping you! And when we say extra cash, we aren't talking about a few hundred bucks. Think $5,000 and above.

Another thing to remember is that there are often different groups of investors for each production, and just because you invested in the Broadway production of *Memphis* does not mean you automatically get a share in the tour profits without investing again. This is more advanced than we have time to explore here, but know that if you missed an opportunity to invest in a Broadway show, you might get a second crack when the tour goes out.

Of course it goes without saying that not every show is a *Hairspray*, *The Producers*, *Jersey Boys*, *Wicked*, or *Book of Mormon* (don't you wish you had invested in one of those?). Roughly 80 percent of shows produced don't make their initial investments back. It is also possible that the show doesn't make its money back on Broadway, but is a cash cow on the road and abroad. As always, you have to do your research on the property and see what its potential is in the marketplace.

Again, Producing/Investing is not limited to theatre. You can get into film, television, or music. Whatever you are passionate about, go do it! With Producing/Investing there are limitless possibilities. At that level you are taking part of the genesis of a project and it is extremely exciting. The slightest ideas in your head can become mega hits with the right team! You can be a part of that, if it is the game you want to play.

Like we said before (and repetition is the mother of all learning), you *must* conduct your due diligence before putting money (yours or anyone else's) anywhere. Is every production or investment going to make you money? No. But the shows that do hit, and hit big, will pay you again and again and again. As the saying goes, "You can't make a living producing Broadway shows, but you can make a *killing!*"

It is a fun game to say the least, but let's now identify some specific pros and cons of being a Producer/Investor.

Some pros:

1. Pure profit! Find yourself a hit show and the world is your oyster. Producers/ Investors of such classics as *Oklahoma!, West Side Story, A Chorus Line, South Pacific, Death of a Salesman, Equus,* or newer box office smashes like *August: Osage County, War Horse, Jersey Boys, Wicked, The Producers, Hairspray,* and *Book of Mormon* will get paid for the rest of their lives every single time that show is performed anywhere!

2. Once your investment is in the black and making money, your work is essentially "over." You will have less to do other than maintaining and building on the success of the production. For example, once *Jersey Boys* was up and running and became one of the hottest tickets in town, the Producers/Investors sat back and watched profits soar as they did their research into the touring and global markets. Needless to say, they are doing just fine! This show will continue to make money for as long as it is open on Broadway or anywhere around the world.

3. There is no limit to how many shows, films, artists, or bands that you can be Producing/Investing in. If you have the funds, time, energy, and passion you can be developing multiple works at the same time. You can even take the profit from one project and roll it into an investment in the next (hopefully) big hit.

4. Once your work is done, there is no need to show up to get paid! Go to bed at night and wake up with more money in the bank. Not a bad deal at all. If you have a huge hit on your hands, you can duplicate the show again and again, in whatever markets you choose.

5. You get to flex your business *and* artistic muscles. This is especially true of Producers, because they are likely to be much more hands-on throughout the project. Investors who make their money in the corporate world yet have always loved the arts get to be a part of putting together something they care deeply about.

Cons:

1. Risk. This is the group that walks some of the most razor-thin edges in show business. Being a Producer/Investor means there is absolutely no safety net. This is not for the fainthearted. That risk is what scares a lot of people away from jumping into this realm. In show business, Producers/Investors are the ones putting thousands, hundreds of thousands, and sometimes millions of their own dollars into mounting a show.

2. If you are not risking your own money, you are risking someone else's money, which can be an even scarier proposition! If you lose a lot of money that was given to you by a corporation or single investor, they are going to be much less likely to invest with you again. Producers have a huge responsibility to their Investors. Their effort is to keep overhead low and profits high so everyone can see a return.

3. No guarantee of income. Producers/Investors can find themselves thinking they had a "sure thing" that would be a big hit on Broadway or on the road, but something goes awry and it doesn't sell. For whatever reason, you are not making what you thought you would. If the show is bleeding money or has zero advance ticket sales, you might have to close your show just weeks or even days after it opens.

A quick word on the ongoing Producer/Actor struggle

Joe & Christine: As actors (and we are aware this is a gross generalization) we tend to look at producers as the greedy money-grubbers who don't care at all about the performers in their show. They sit back and seemingly make oodles of cash, while we do eight shows a week and make the same amount no matter what. They are also the people who, when it comes time to negotiate with our union, always try to whittle our contracts down. This is the perspective that a lot of actors have. However, when you look at things from a non-emotional point of view, it is really just a question of math and capitalism. It is a simple reality that we are dealing with, and once you understand it and make peace with it, everything gets easier. That reality is that every employer, everywhere in the world, wants the same exact thing. They want to get as much quality work out of their employees as they possibly can and pay them as little as they possibly can, while charging as much as they possibly can for their product. Ask any business owner, or producer, or whomever, and they will all tell you the same thing. That is not to say they don't care about their employees, or that they aren't willing to pay top dollar for top talent, but they do want to pay as little top dollar as they have to. I haven't met a producer yet who is complaining that they aren't paying their people enough! And any employee, anywhere in the world, is going to want the same thing as well, only reversed. They want to be paid as much as they possibly can, for doing as little work as they possibly can. You have to look at show business the same way: The key word is show business!

"If 'show business' were not a business it would be called 'show show.'"
– Woody Allen

(Continued):

Take away the good guy/bad guy element and you just have a case of everyone wanting to make as much money as they can. We say this because when things come up with contract negotiations and salaries/benefits are on the table, it is easy for an Actor to get very angry with the Producer/Investor for wanting to pay him less. But going in knowing how the business world works, and accepting it as part of the game, takes the animosity out of the entire process. That is not to say that we as Actors shouldn't go in and negotiate tooth and nail for as much as we can... this is, after all, our livelihood we are talking about here. We believe that if you are going to play a game, then you'd better play to win. It doesn't mean that the other side has to "lose"; it just means that as a trained and skilled professional, it is OK to demand a high premium on your talent. Your product (you) is only worth what you are willing to sell it for.

Chapter 7 - The Money Talk - Part 2
Becoming an "Artist-preneur"

Now that we have covered the main areas of how show business income is generated we would like to illustrate a few real-world examples of artists who started in one group, and then combined or switched as their career developed.

From ACTOR to STAR/SPECIALTY

We see this happen when an Actor lands her first leading role in a new show. She gets nominated and maybe even wins a Tony® Award. It's a dream come true! These Actors now have the opportunity, if they choose, to put together a one-person show or do a cabaret performance of songs they love and perform as a Star/Specialty. They may even take it as far as booking several dates and doing a small tour. They use the momentum they built from being an Actor to propel their Star/Specialty act. People who have successfully made this transition (and back again) include Patti LuPone, Mandy Patinkin, Brian Stokes Mitchell, Norm Lewis, and Bernadette Peters, just to name a few. They will fill their "down time" with concerts and solo acts and eventually they cross groups with ease.

Joe: I was in The Little Mermaid *on Broadway with Norm Lewis and there were times when he would take a day or two off from playing the role of King Triton in our show to go and do a concert as a featured soloist. Since the show closed in the fall of 2009, he has done a lot of concert work as his "day job," in addition to starring in two other Broadway shows since then! Sherie Rene Scott is another example of an artist going from Actor to Star/Specialty with her show* Everyday Rapture.

From ACTOR to CREATOR/WRITER

A voice-over artist can have multiple campaigns airing at the same time. Let's say they did a spot for Prilosec and one for Pepsi. Once they do the work, they sit back and watch the checks roll in while they audition for their next voice-over. They are Actors who become similar to Creators/Writers because they got paid a session fee for the recording (wage) but now do not have to show up every day to get paid (residual profit). Actors who work regularly on a series like *Law & Order*, or films/commercials, earn residual income in the same way. They are paid for the day, and then paid again every time the show/film/commercial is run. Each Actor/Creator/Writer combination did the work, got paid for it, and then continues to get paid over time. Is all this starting to make sense?

Joe: An example of an actor working in three groups happened again while I was in The Little Mermaid. I sat in the dressing room next to a wonderful actor named Robert Creighton, or "Bobby C." for short. Bobby had always wanted to do a show about James Cagney because he loved his work and knew (rightly so) that he was perfect to play the title role. Since there wasn't a show about him to date, Bobby got together with some partners and they wrote it. Now you can see where this is going right? Bobby had been developing that show off and on for several years, and eventually his show, titled Cagney! *was picked up by a theater in Florida and was going to be produced for the first time. He did the show to rave reviews and set box office records for that theater (congrats again, Bobby!). Using that momentum, he is working to get his show produced in several theaters around the country. In this instance, Bobby has operated in three of the four groups in which artists can work. He performed in the show (Actor), it was a show written specifically for him (Star/ Specialty), and as it gets produced in other places he is earning money (Creator/ Writer), because he obviously won't be in every production around the country. Bobby essentially got paid three times for doing one show. Bobby wouldn't stay permanently in the Star/Specialty group, because he knew that he wanted to get the show out to several theaters at once. He was smart enough to write a show that was perfect for him, but not so much so that he was the only person who could play the role of James Cagney. Now he can play the role when he wants to, and when he is otherwise obligated, he can hire another actor to play the part, but as the Creator/ Writer, Bobby will still get paid.*

From ACTOR to PRODUCER/INVESTOR

As Actors work more and continue to build their networks, they are bound to include those who are already doing a lot of Producing/Investing. Actors simply let them know they are interested in Producing/Investing and see what projects they have access to. Sometimes Actors will connect with people who are at the very beginning stages of raising money and the minimum investment is as high as $100,000 or even $250,000. As time goes on, that minimum amount will get smaller as they open it up to smaller individual investors, and that is when Actors can possibly jump in.

Obviously there are lots of other combinations as to how you can change your "grouping" in the business. Going from an Actor to Creator/Writer happens when you write your own show, perhaps star in it, then license it out to be done in several locations. From Creator/Writer to Producer/Investor can happen when you write a successful show, and then take the ongoing profits and invest in new works.

Looking at all of the examples above, you should now have a very clear idea as to what "group" you are in at the moment. The thing to remember is that the residual income is made by the Creator/Writers and Producer/Investors. They do the work once and continue to earn on it over and over again. The people who have to show up to get paid are the Actors and Star/Specialties. You may be very well compensated for your work, however when you don't show up or when the show closes, you *stop* getting paid.

Maybe you never really thought about creating your own show or investing in a show, or maybe you did. We hope that after reading this section, you can see how you can be satisfied artistically and financially. Being a Thriving Artist means having multiple streams of income flowing. We always want you to operate from a place of choice and freedom, rather than restriction and desperation.

The point of this section on the economic landscape of show business was to illustrate the different ways of how you, as an artist, can make money. Knowing what the possibilities are, and the pros and cons of each, will arm you with more financial awareness as you move through your career. Two groups are trading time for money (Actors and Star/Specialties), and two of them lead to residual income (Creator/Writer and Producer/Investor). What game do you want to play?

PERFORMING ON BROADWAY = THE FINANCIAL HOLY GRAIL...OR MAYBE NOT.

We can't tell you how many times we have heard, "If I could just land a Broadway show, all of my money troubles would be over." Or "I will start saving once I get a production contract." News flash: If you don't know how to manage what money you have, how are you ever going to manage more of it? (Insert sirens and flashing lights here!) There is a reason why a lot of lottery winners are broke after just a few short years after they won millions of dollars. Overnight they have gobs of cash and none of the financial knowledge needed to go along with it, yet they thought it was the answer to all their prayers. As the saying goes, "Money doesn't come with instructions." They buy homes, cars, take expensive vacations, and when the bills start coming in, they don't have the money to pay. It's very sad. We do not want artists to be in the same boat. *Financial education needs to happen before you land that big job;* then saving even more money and taking it to the next level by making it work for you will be a cinch. You will easily be able to budget for whatever it is that you want. We will say this many times: The financial decision(s) you make or *do not make* early on your life or career will affect you for the rest of your life. We don't want any regrets.

We have been lucky enough to make a Broadway paycheck for several years and it is truly a wonderful thing, but it is not the end-all-be-all of income, because eventually, the show will close. The question is, will you be in a better financial position than you were before the show started? This is one of the main points of being a Thriving Artist. Personally speaking, we are in this game to have long and prosperous careers, not just one show and a couple years in the city, and then moving back to our hometown. There is nothing wrong with having a few fun years in NY, LA or wherever, and then moving back home, if that was your plan all along. But, if show business *is* your long-term career choice, then this should open your eyes a bit. Even if you are going home to work a job outside of show business, the principles in this book will help give you a working financial knowledge and put you on the right track, no matter where your paycheck comes from.

TIME FOR A BREAKDOWN
You have chosen a profession in which the top earning potential for an ensemble member on Broadway is $1,754 a week (at the time of this publication). This of course is not the case if you're one of the leads in a Broadway show. Principals usually make a great deal more and are on a different type of contract.

So, $1,754 is the Broadway minimum for anyone in the chorus. This is the top ensemble salary for the theatre, not taking into account increases for understudy pay, specialties, hazard pay, and the like. However, we will just break down the minimum paycheck for simplification.

Let's crunch some numbers:

This is to give you an idea of what to expect from your paycheck as an actor with or without debt.

Broadway minimum: $1,754 (as of this writing)

Federal taxes for you will be between 15 – 25 percent of your income, depending on your filing status and the number of deductions/exemptions you make to lower your taxable income.

Current 2013 brackets for annual income when filing as a single taxpayer are as follows:

$0 - $8,925	=	10% tax bracket
$8,926 - $36,250	=	15% tax bracket
$36,251 - $87,850	=	25% tax bracket
$87,751 - $183,250	=	28% tax bracket
$183,251 - $398,350	=	33% tax bracket
$398,351 - above	=	35% tax bracket

Current 2013 brackets for annual income when married filing jointly are:

$0 - $17,850	=	10% tax bracket
$17,851 - $72,500	=	15% tax bracket
$72,501 - $146,400	=	25% tax bracket
$146,401 - $223,050	=	28% tax bracket
$223,051 - $398,350	=	33% tax bracket
$398,351 - $450,000	=	35% tax bracket
$450,001 - above	=	39.6% tax bracket

(For ease of example we will continue with the single person's income.)

Working on Broadway, you will be in the 28% tax bracket because the government taxes you using $1,754 as your weekly income. This being the case, your gross annual income is approximately $91,208. Your actual *taxable income* may be lower than this after you take your deductions at the end of the year.

(Note: Tax rates and laws can, and often do, change every year. The below percentages are for example only and may become inaccurate as time goes on, however, they are likely to be +/- a few percentage points so the example remains relevant. Also, the graduated federal tax and graduated New York state/city taxes are calculated on a progressive scale. What that means is when taxable income falls within a particular tax bracket, the individual pays the listed percentage of tax on each dollar that falls within that monetary range. For example, a person who earns $10,000 of taxable income in 2013 (income after adjustments, deductions, and exemptions) would be liable for 10% of each dollar earned from the 1st dollar to the 8,925th dollar, and then for 15% of each dollar earned from the 8,926th dollar to the 10,000th dollar. So the total tax on $10,000 would be $1,053.75 rather than $1,500, even though that income is in the 15% tax bracket.)

The following are your *per paycheck* deductions, assuming the 28% tax bracket:

Federal income tax at 28% is **$365.36**

Social Security tax (plus Medicare) at 7.65% is **$134.18**

New York state tax (if you make over $20,000) at 6.65% is **$107.67**

New York City tax (based on income level) at 3.648% is **$61.72**

Actors' Equity Union dues at 2.25% is **$39.46**

Your take-home pay is now **$1,045.61/week**

If you have an agent, he/she will take 10 percent of your gross weekly income so that would be another $175.40 coming out of your check automatically every week. This is also before you put money into your 401(k), which also comes out of your gross income. Both of these, while necessary, will lower your take-home pay (but not as much as you might think). We will talk about this in later chapters.

But let's say for these purposes that you don't have an agent and you now have $1,045.61 to work with.

We now have to factor in your necessities. These are not set in stone, but we will figure on the low side because you just moved to NYC and chose to live in an outer borough like Queens or Brooklyn. These figures are not based on splitting your utilities, TV, Internet bills, etc. with roommates. We can factor that in later when we talk about where to live.

You have **$1,045.61/week ($4182.44 per month)**

Rent is **$175/week ($700 per month)**

Utility (electric and gas) bill is **$20/week ($80 per month)**

Cell phone bill is **$20/week ($80 per month)**

A monthly unlimited subway pass **is $28/week ($112 per month)**

TV/Internet bill is around **$30/week ($120 per month)**

Food is **$75/week ($300 per month)**

Your weekly net is now **$697.61 ($2790.44 per month)**

If your school loan is $300 a month, that takes another $75/week out of your check.

Your weekly net (after school loan payment) is now **$622.61 ($2490.44 per month)**

We will assume you don't have a car loan or any credit card debt, and we will also not factor in any dance classes or voice lessons. We are keeping with the bare minimums for this example.

To clear **$622.61** after expenses per week is great, but we made a lot of assumptions here. As the costs of college have increased, most school loan payments are not just $300. Christine's school loan payment at the time (which was a few years back J) was $286 a month and she only owed $17,000 total. Many school loans these days are for substantially more money.

This is also sticking to only $75 a week for food. You can easily spend that in a meal or two with a glass of wine. This $622.61 per week is also before you see one movie, a Broadway show, or buy toothpaste. This is before you pay anywhere from $85 to $125 an hour for a voice lesson with a good teacher. We are also assuming you have health insurance through the union. If you qualify for that, you will have to pay a minimum of $400 per year for your premiums, along with the $25 co-pay for every doctor visit. If you need any prescriptions you will have to first meet your deductible, which can be as much as a few hundred dollars before your insurance covers your medication. Recent developments with health care now dictate that if you do not qualify for health insurance with the union (or other employer), you will have to pay anywhere from $100 to $400 per month for coverage. Also, most people who share rent (even with a roommate) pay over $700 a month. It is often closer to $800 to $900 a month.

The point of all this is not to scare you, but to give you some real-world numbers to go by. People tend to think that their Broadway show will be the answer to all their financial prayers, and like we said, it is a wonderful thing…just not *every-thing*. If you have *any* debt (school loans, credit cards, car loan) you may be in for a rude awakening when you sit down and do your finances after you graduate from school. Mom and Dad probably won't be paying for things anymore. If they are helping you that is great and you should count your blessings, but one day it will end and we want you to be ready when it does.

So let's run the numbers again with higher rent, a higher school loan payment, higher cost for food, agent commission, voice lessons, and a gym membership. In our opinion, this is closer to what people's expenses typically are.

Your gross salary is **$1,754** per week.

After taxes (same 28% rate as previous example) and 10 percent agent fee your new net weekly salary is **$870.21**

We will up your rent to **$200/week ($800 per month)**

Utilities (electric and gas) bill is **$20/week ($80 per month)**

Cell phone bill is **$20/week ($80 per month)**

Monthly unlimited subway pass is **$28/week ($112 per month)**

TV/Internet bill is around **$30/week ($120 per month)**

Food is **$100/week ($400 per month)**

School loan payment is **$100/week ($400 per month)**

Gym membership is **$15/week ($60 per month)**

Voice lessons are approximately $85 each and you take two a month = **$42.50/week ($170 per month)**

After all of these expenses, you now have **$314.71** per week in your pocket. Again, this is before you buy toothpaste, see a movie, or have a night on the town. Big difference, huh? Again, this is not to scare you, just a close look at reality.

Believe us, we want you to go to the gym. Please continue to take voice lessons and train across all disciplines of your art! What the numbers above illustrate is that while the Broadway paycheck is a beautiful thing, it is not the genie to grant all your financial wishes. While keeping yourself on a budget, however, you *can* save/invest as much as **$1,258.84** per month or **$15,106.08** per year. That can make a difference when invested wisely, and that is exactly what a Thriving Artist working on Broadway would do (*in addition to generating money from other income streams*).

Of course the above numbers are not absolute and there is leeway in all expense areas. Maybe you will not have a school loan and perhaps your other bills will be shared as well. The point to keep in mind is that no matter what the contract/job you are working, the intention is always to finish it in a better financial position than when you started. Knowing what your expenses are and sticking to a budget can really have a positive financial impact in the long run. The financial decisions you make in your early years/career will really have a lasting effect on your life!

"Please avoid being young, fabulous, on Broadway…and broke!"
- Joe & Christine

Saving or investing money as seen in the above example can easily be done. The mistake that many artists make is that as soon as they land their Broadway show, series regular, or other big job, they ditch Woodside, Queens, or Washington Heights and head for the Upper West Side of Manhattan (or they leave the Valley for West Hollywood…insert your suburbs-to-downtown reference here!). Now their monthly rent is likely to be $1,000 or more, they tend to eat out all the time, and they start to buy gadgets they don't necessarily need - because hey, they are young, fabulous, and on Broadway! Again, we are not saying that you don't deserve an iPad or other fancy toy. But don't buy the iPad, a new 50" flat screen, an Xbox One, and a fancy Marc Jacobs bag all at the same time. Catch our drift?

Joe: While I was in the Broadway company of Hairspray, *the Local 1 Stagehand Union in New York went on strike. The strike lasted for nineteen days and upon returning to work there were cast members talking about how much financial trouble they were in, because we weren't getting paid our Broadway salary while the strike was on. (We were able to collect New York State unemployment compensation though.) That is more understandable for someone brand-new to the show or fresh to NYC, however, these particular cast members who were complaining about financial hardship had been in the show for well over a year! I remember people talking about taking out a loan from the bank to pay bills! What had they been doing with their money all this time? It was only nineteen days without work! I am not saying this to beat anybody up or to put anyone down. I am saying it out of surprise and out of caring for my fellow cast mates. Please don't let that happen to you! Hard times may come in your career, but having hard times financially <u>while you are working</u> is something that is 100 percent avoidable. Be smart!*

Please don't give in to peer pressure or conform to the "cool" kids who think Manhattan is the *only* place to live. The world does not begin or end with Manhattan and don't listen to anyone who says it does. You will be the "cool" kid when you afford that gorgeous house in a few years and spend your weekends in the country.

"Entrepreneurship is living a few years of your life like most people won't, so that you can spend the rest of your life like most people can't."
- Anonymous

The decisions that you make today that will shape your financial future for tomorrow. You may think that the extra $300 per month in rent to live in Manhattan does not matter today, but if you were to get a long-running Broadway show and could save that $300 each month, what might your financial future look like? If you save an extra $300 per month, that adds up to $3,600 for one year. If your show runs for two years, now you have pocketed $7,200. Three years is $10,800, just by staying in your cheaper apartment. The math looks like this: if you invest $286 every month starting at twenty-five years old, assuming an average 8 percent annual return, you will have a million dollars by the time you reach sixty-five years old. Would that make a difference in your retirement?

Now you may be asking yourself, "How in the heck can I guarantee an 8 percent return?" The answer is, you can't guarantee it. But you *can* give yourself a better shot at hitting the million-dollar mark by reading the next section.

Be patient, keep getting educated, and stick to your plan. Take the financial road less travelled by most artists. You will be very thankful you did.

Chapter 8 – Money Management Specifics
The How-To of Asset Creation

"I spent a lot of money on booze, birds, and fast cars.
The rest I just squandered."
- George Best

Joe: When I was in college, all I could think about was getting to Broadway…it was what made me get up in the morning and go to that 8 a.m. sight-singing class and it's what made me stay late and work for an extra hour after most of my dance classes. I hope you share the same passion I have for doing this amazing work. But what do you do once you get that job and are getting paid every week?

You are making money, now what? We keep talking about saving/investing money and what you can financially do in a year, or two, or three. But we all know, or at least somewhat understand by this point in this book, that money lying in a savings account probably isn't the best way to make it grow. So, how *do* you make money grow?

There are several levels to answering this question. For the purposes of this book, we are going to start with a focus on what to do with your income from whatever job(s) you have.

> *Disclaimer:*
> *WE ARE NOT RECOMMENDING THE SPECIFIC PURCHASE AND/ OR INVESTMENT INTO ANY OF THE FINANCIAL PRODUCTS MENTIONED BELOW. WE ARE SIMPLY USING THEM AS AN ILLUSTRATION AND EMPHASIZING THAT IT IS IMPORTANT TO GET EDUCATED ABOUT WHAT IS AVAILABLE, WHAT THESE PRODUCTS CAN DO, AND THEN TO MAKE YOUR OWN DECISIONS. WE ARE NOT, NOR DO WE CLAIM TO BE, FINANCIAL EXPERTS. WE ARE SIMPLY RELAYING WHAT WE HAVE LEARNED AND HOW THESE VARIOUS INVESTMENT VEHICLES HAVE WORKED FOR US IN THE FINANCIAL SUCCESS WE HAVE HAD THUS FAR.*

That said, here is a list of things that we have done with the money we have made from performance work.

SPECIFIC MONEY MANAGEMENT ACTIONS

Taking an active role in managing your money is a *must* for every Thriving Artist. Over the years we have used the systems we are about to show you. Now that you have some money coming in, it's time to learn the skills needed to make the most of it.

THRIVING ARTISTS MONEY MASTERY TALENTS

MASTERY #1. APPRECIATE: What is your context for money? When we start the statement, "Money is..." how would you finish it? Take some time to think about that, because it is the most important financial skill to have and everything else builds on it. Make sure that however you finish that sentence, you are creating a *positive* context for money in your life. Remember from earlier in this book: If you have the context of a coffee cup, you are not going to put champagne into it. They just don't go together. So make sure that your context is one of putting great value and appreciation on money. The Universe will not provide you with something you do not consciously value highly, so make sure to clear out any negativity or old programming. We want you to receive all that you are deserving of and a proper context for money can help do that for you. Master the art of appreciation.

MASTERY #2. GENERATE: We talked about this in the "Payable Skills" section earlier. As Thriving Artists, we are constantly creating new streams of income that pay us financially as well as emotionally. Being miserable, but making a lot of money, is *not* what we are all about...we're sure you get that by now. Along with those new ways of making money, we are also looking for leverage and how we can make that a residual asset. There are twenty-four hours in the day and we have only so much energy to give. However, with a great team, which creates leverage, true wealth can be generated. Master the art of creative income generation.

MASTERY #3. KEEP: We will tell you, as most financial experts will, that *you must pay yourself first*. What does that mean? It means that you take a percentage of your weekly check (after taxes) and you put it away where you cannot touch it. We like third-party online bank accounts, such as Emigrant Direct or Capitol One 360, which offer a higher interest rate and can easily be connected to your personal checking/savings account. Virtually every bank is FDIC insured so your money is safe up to (currently) $250,000.

The object is to have your money work for you, even in your savings account. We all love having money saved, because it tends to makes us feel safer and more secure. Most financial advisors recommend having at least three months of your living expenses in your savings account (we believe you really should have closer to six months saved if possible). This means if something should happen you would have enough money to cover rent, food, utilities, and incidentals for at least three to six months. Three months can go by in a flash, and you might not be back on your feet yet, so six months seems more sensible in our estimation.

Now, it doesn't matter what percentage you allot to this savings fund, but what *does* matter is that you do it like clockwork. In the best of all worlds you take 10 percent of your after-tax paycheck and put it away every single week. As we are writing this book, the interest rates for savings and/or checking accounts are less than 2 percent. The interest rate does not matter as much as the *discipline* of saving does! Start now. Master the art of keeping your money.

MASTERY #4. GROW: (Note: This is a very long section packed with information. Take your time and digest as much as you can before going on.) Here is where things get interesting. There are *a lot* of options out there when it comes to investing and we are not going to even scratch the surface of what you potentially can do. Much like saving your money, the percentage that you invest is not as important as the discipline of doing it. We'll talk quite a bit about the 401(k) plan (because it is what we have the most experience with) and other options as well, but this is where you need to do a lot of your own digging. Find out what interests you, see what works for you, and then do it. *Again, this is a long section so please stick with us.* Let's begin.

There are three basic types of investment accounts you can set up. A good analogy is to think of these accounts like different houses, each with different "house rules." The specific funds, stocks, bonds, etc. where your money is invested are like the rooms in that particular house. We will not be covering each of them in great detail, but we will be offering enough information to at least familiarize you with what they are. Our effort is to shine a light on some things that perhaps you never knew you didn't know, and in the process inspire you to do some more exploration of the topic.

Investment Account #1 – The 401(k)

Definition of a 401(k): In the United States, a 401(k) retirement savings plan allows a worker to save for retirement and have the savings invested while deferring current income taxes on the saved money and earnings until withdrawal. It is a retirement savings account offered by employers only. Individuals cannot invest in a 401(k) unless it is through an employer.

(Note: There are stringent rules for withdrawal. If withdrawal is made before the age of fifty-nine and a half, there are tax implications in addition to a 10 percent early withdrawal penalty. Please check with your personal tax advisor for specific details).

Contributing somewhere between 5 percent and 15 percent to a 401(k) is what is usually recommended. That may seem like a lot of your check going into Never-Never Land, but remember, 401(k) contributions go into your fund *before* Uncle Sam takes his cut in taxes. This lowers your taxable income and allows you to more effectively pay yourself first. Ultimately it does not drastically affect your post-tax dollars.

> An important note: If your employer contributes to your 401(k) only if you do, and you don't take advantage of this, you are missing out. It's "free money" that you are leaving on the table. Once you opt in, the employer will contribute whatever percentage the company has set aside toward your retirement, and all you have to do is contribute a percentage of your salary as well. Some companies will actually match what you elect to contribute so it literally doubles your money. It really won't make that much difference in your paycheck. Do the math and you'll see.

As actors we are lucky. Currently, if you work a production contract, the producers contribute 3 percent into your fund whether you do or not! If you contribute just 3 percent of your salary, you are now getting a total of 6 percent contribution every week. Who wouldn't want to invest one dollar and get credit for two?

This next section comes directly from the Actors' Equity website's Members Only section:

(Note: If you are an artist who is not in show business at all you may want to skip this section, although we recommend reading it for educational purposes.)

The following contracts allow for 401(k) employer *and* deferral contributions: Production Contract (Equity/League) and Production Contract (Disney Theatrical Productions, Ltd). These employers currently contribute 3 percent of your weekly compensation up to a maximum contribution of $225 per week, based on the maximum weekly salary cap of $7,500. The maximum single employer contribution to an actor/stage manager for the year 2013 is $7,500.

Many Equity contracts that do not have an employer contribution will now allow you to make your own contribution into a 401(k) plan each week, which is deducted from your weekly salary.

What type of contract do I have to be working under in order to be able to participate in the 401(k) Plan?

There are two types of Equity-League 401(k) plans: one type offers salary deferral only, while the other offers both salary and employer contributions.

SALARY DEFERRAL AND EMPLOYER CONTRIBUTIONS
Equity/League Production Contract
Equity/Disney Theatrical Ventures, Inc. Production Contract
League of Resident Theatres (LORT)
WCLO (Western Civic Light Opera) Contract
University/Resident Theatre (URTA) Agreement

SALARY DEFERRAL ONLY
Off Broadway Contract
COST (Council of Stock Theatres) Contract
Special Production Contract
White Christmas-Special Agreements
City Center Encores-Special Agreement
Menopause Special Agreements
Mid-Size Theatres

Chanhassen Dinner Theatres; Chanhassen, MN

Beef & Boards Dinner Theatre; Indianapolis, IN

New Theatre Restaurant; Overland Park, KS

Drury Lane Theatre; Oakbrook, IL

Drury Lane Water Tower; Chicago, IL

American Heartland Theatre; Kansas City, MO

Marriott Theatre; Lincolnshire, IL

Casino Contracts

RMTA (Resident Musical Theatre Association)

CAT (Chicago Area Theatres Contract)

Musical Stock and Unit Attractions MSUA Contract

Outdoor Drama Contract

TYA (Theatre for Young Audiences) Contract

Business Theatre and Events Contract

Second City Agreement (Chicago, Detroit, Las Vegas)

Children's Theatre Company

Bay Area Theatre (BAT)

Ellis Island Foundations

Lawrence Welk Resort Dinner Theatre

Westchester Broadway Dinner Theatre

Alhambra Dinner Theatre; Jacksonville, FL

City Center Summer Stars-Special Agreement

ANTC (Association of Non-Profit Theatre Companies)

Walt Disney World; Orlando, FL

New Candlelight Dinner Theatre

CORST (Council of Resident Stock Theatres)

DORA the Explorer – Special Agreement

Cabaret Agreement

What is the maximum salary per week that may be used to calculate contributions?

The maximum salary per week that may be used to calculate contributions is $7,500. Salary includes contractual salary, overtime, unused vacation, unused sick leave, and over scale expense payments and per diems.

What is the producer's contribution to the 401(k) Plan while working under a Production Contract?

The producer will contribute an amount equal to 3 percent of your weekly compensation up to a maximum contribution of $225 per week. This is based on the maximum weekly salary of $7,500 times the employer contribution of 3 percent.

Can I defer or contribute part of my own salary into the Plan?

For the 2011 plan year, if you are working under the Production Contract you may choose to defer up to 85 percent of your weekly salary up to a maximum of $6,375 per week. This is based on the maximum weekly salary of $7,500 times the maximum deferral of 85 percent. You may change these contributions at any time or you may choose not to defer any part of your salary. This contribution is called a Deferred Salary Contribution.

The Internal Revenue Service (IRS) limits the amount of salary you can defer to this or any other plan on a tax-deferred basis. In 2013, the annual limit is $17,500. Note that if you are fifty or older you are eligible to defer an additional $5,500 for the year 2013.

Can I defer or contribute to the 401(k) Plan from over scale per diem?

Deferred Salary Contributions can only be made from taxable income. If you are being paid expenses you can only make deferrals from taxable over scale per diem.

What is the maximum contribution per year per employer?

The federal government limits the maximum amount of annual compensation, per employer, that can be taken into account for determining contributions for a participant under a qualified plan. For the year 2013 this amount is $255,000. The maximum employer contribution of 3 percent for an actor and or stage manager for the year 2013 is $7,650 (3 percent of $255,000).

What is the maximum amount of salary that I can defer to the 401(k) Plan per year?

The Internal Revenue Service limits the amount of salary you can defer to this or any other plan on a tax-deferred basis. In 2013, the annual limit is $17,500. Note that if you are fifty or older you are eligible to defer an additional $5,500 for the year 2013.

What are the tax implications of contributing to the 401(k) Plan?

Federal income taxes are deferred for all monies contributed to the 401(k) Plan, as well as the interest earned. State income taxes are also deferred with the exception of state income taxes for the State of Pennsylvania. Pennsylvania will deduct state income taxes prior to any deferrals to the 401(k) Plan. In addition, Medicare and Social Security taxes are not deferred. To find out how this will affect your personal finances you must contact your personal tax advisor.

Can I voluntarily contribute to the 401(k) Plan after taxes?

No. You must be employed by any of the contracts that are eligible under the plan and all salary deferrals must be before taxes are taken out.

Can I rollover into my Equity-League 401(k) Plan funds from another retirement plan?

Yes. You may rollover funds from a qualified retirement plan into your 401(k) Plan. You may download the 'Rollover Statement' from the website or you may contact the Fund Office.

Rollovers are accepted from plans qualified under Section 401(a) or 403(a) (excluding after-tax employee contributions) an annuity contract described in section 403(b), an eligible plan under section 457(b) of the Code that is maintained by a state, political subdivision of a state, or any agency, or instrumentality of a state or political subdivision of a state, or from IRAs under 408(a) or (b). Roth IRAs are not eligible for rollover into your Equity-League 401(k) Plan.

Can I withdraw the funds from my Equity-League 401(k) Plan and roll them over into another retirement plan?

Yes. You are eligible to withdraw your account balance if:

- You reach normal retirement age (fifty-nine and a half), or

- You are not employed for twelve months under any collective bargaining agreement, allowing for deferrals to this plan and are not so employed when you apply for withdrawal of your account,

- You are permanently and totally disabled (as defined by the Plan)

Who is the Actors Equity 401(k) Plan's provider?

MassMutual Retirement Services is the Plan's Provider.

What are my investment options?

MassMutual offers you twenty-two investment options:

> You can direct the investment of your contributions in increments of 1 percent of your portfolio to any or all of the investment funds available under the Plan. MassMutual currently offers you the following twenty-two investment options, however, the options are subject to change. Please refer to the MassMutual website for specific fund prospectus information.

Default Investment Option

> If you do not give instructions as to how to invest your account, or if contributions are received before you give such instructions, your contributions will be invested in the Manning and Napier Retirement Target-date option that is appropriate for you, based upon your current age and the assumption that you will retire at age sixty-five. This is the default investment vehicle under the Plan. If the Fund Office does not have your date of birth on file, and you have not given investment instructions, your account will be invested in the Manning and Napier Target Income Series.

If any portion of your account balance was defaulted in the Manning and Napier Target Income Funds, you may always direct future contributions to any of the investment options available and transfer any amounts already defaulted.

How can I change my investment options?

MassMutual will provide you with a pin number, which will enable you to change your investment options via a toll-free number or Internet site.

When am I vested?

Vesting is immediate and at 100 percent.

(Note: In layman's terms "vested" means that you have full ownership and rights to the stock, money, equity, etc., that you own or have invested in. Sometimes, for example with stock options as part of an employee's compensation, those shares are not available to that employee until a certain date in the future. He or she is not "vested" in those shares yet. When that date does arrive he/she then has access to those shares (money). In this case with the Actors Equity 401(k) plan, you are vested immediately in whatever fund you choose. You do not have to wait to "own" that money you've invested.)

Are Hardship Withdrawals available under the Plan?

Yes. Effective January 1, 2005, Hardship Withdrawals have been added to the 401(k) plan. If you encounter a hardship situation that is based on the following conditions that have been defined by the IRS, and the Plan, then you will qualify for this withdrawal

- Expenses for medical care for yourself, spouse, or dependent.

- Purchase of primary residence excluding mortgage payments.

- Tuition and related education fees including room and board expenses, for the next twelve months for post-secondary education for yourself, spouse, or dependent.

- Prevention of eviction or foreclosure on your primary residence.

- Funeral expenses of parents, spouse, children, or dependents.

- Certain expenses relating to the repair of damage to the employee's principal residence such as hurricane or flood damage.

To apply, please contact the 401(k) Department at the New York Office for an application.

If the hardship withdrawal is approved, your eligibility to defer a portion of your salary into the Plan will be suspended for six months.

When am I eligible to withdraw or rollover my account balance?

You are eligible to withdraw or rollover your account balance if:

- You reach normal retirement age (fifty-nine and a half)

- You are not employed for twelve months under any collective bargaining agreement allowing for deferrals to this plan and are not so employed when you apply for withdrawal of your account

- You are permanently and totally disabled (as defined by the Plan)

- You qualify for a Hardship Withdrawal (as defined by the IRS). Please note Hardship Withdrawals are not eligible for rollovers.

How can I take the distribution of my account balance once I retire?

You may receive your account balance in one lump sum or you may withdraw partial lump sums.

What happens to my 401(k) Plan if I die before collecting any part of it?

If you die, your account will be paid as a death benefit under the rules of the Plan.

If I am incorporated (employed as a corporation), can I still participate in the 401(k) Plan?

Actors employed through corporations will be eligible for employer contributions however; they will not be eligible for salary deferrals.

What are the Plan's expenses?

The Plan has to pay for its administrative expenses, such as salaries, rent and postage. The Plan also has to pay a fee to its service provider, MassMutual. The Trustees make every effort to keep the costs of the Plan as low as possible.

Will I receive two quarterly statements from MassMutual if I am or was receiving employer and/or deferral contributions under a Production contract, and now only receiving deferral contributions while working under a contract that only permits deferral and not employer contributions, for example, Off-Broadway?

No, you will receive one quarterly investment statement from MassMutual. All of your contributions will be consolidated into one account in order to invest these monies accordingly. If you have any questions regarding your 401(k) account, please contact the Retirement Services Department for assistance.

We know this is a lot of information, but it is essential that you are aware of your investment opportunities.

We have worked many of those other contracts where you (the Actor) can contribute to your 401(k) account when the producer does not. Why would you contribute when your employer doesn't? The answer is simple: *to save more money and pay yourself first.* We are not saying that the 401(k) is the best of all investment vehicles, but it is a good place to start as long as *you are actively involved with managing it!* There isn't a retirement plan, mutual fund, stock, bond, or any investment product that can be left on autopilot. You must get educated and you must get in the game.

Christine: I wanted more money in my 401(k) account, but I hadn't worked a Production Contract in a while, where the producer's contributions are automatic. Unfortunately, you can only contribute to your Actors' Equity-sponsored 401(k) while you are working an AEA job so I chose to take part of my salary from a regional job and put it into my 401(k). If you would like to put your saved money elsewhere, by all means, go for it. But you must save. I also like the idea of lowering my taxable income, because 401(k) contributions come from the gross rather than the net income. I want my money in my pocket now, so I can aggressively grow it. I'd rather not give the government an interest-free loan on me.

If that last statement "not give the government an interest-free loan" is unfamiliar to you, here is a brief clarification: When taxes are taken out of your weekly paycheck, that is the federal government taking its "share" of your money to pay for the cost of running the country. When you fill out your tax forms each year, you are telling the government how much you should have paid in taxes, based on your income and your tax-deductible spending. The difference between what you paid and what you should have paid is the money that comes back to you in your tax return, or that you might owe if you kept too much from each check. Essentially, if you have a large tax return check that comes to you every year that means you overpaid your taxes, and the government had use of your money all year. The catch is that they return it to you free of interest! So you have effectively given Uncle Sam an interest-free loan, when that money could have been working and growing for you. Some people like getting a large check every year and consider it to be "found money." We would rather have that money in our control so we can make the most of it all year, but that choice is completely up to you.

A word of caution: Some people believe that 401(k) plans, or any mutual fund for that matter, are the be-all and end-all of investing. They are not, and putting the money in either a 401(k) or any fund is just one step in the process. Once your money is in a fund, you must be very diligent about where it is going and how it is performing. You cannot assume that your investment is doing well or that you don't need to think about it. Quite the opposite is true. Pay attention and keep track of what is happening out there. Too many people lost way too much of their portfolio value when the market crashed in 2008. <u>Protect your investments, because nobody else will care about them as much as you!</u>

Christine: Early in my investing life I was one of those people described above. At first, I didn't watch my investments like I should have. I had money in a Roth IRA, a 401(k), and some CDs. Unfortunately, I was betting my retirement on someone else's due diligence. When I first started my 401(k) in 2001, I was investing around 12 percent, because that is what the representative from MassMutual told me I should do. I was also a good student and put it in a moderate risk/reward investment like the nice man in the suit advised me to. As a woman, who is statistically going to outlive her husband, chances are I could tolerate a little risk in my financial life. Boy, if that isn't a generalization, I don't know what is! Well, as it turned out, keeping my money there was <u>not</u> the best decision for me, and it did not perform like I needed it to. Compared to other clients with a lot more money than me, I didn't get much attention. It wasn't until years later that I took more control and, while nobody can predict the future, my money is doing much better now that I am paying close attention to it.

Now, is putting your money in your 401(k) and not paying much attention to it better than not investing in your retirement at all? Maybe. But that is not the Thriving Artists way at all! Like we said, no one, and we mean *no one*, will be as attentive to your money as you. Mr. or Mrs. Mutual Fund Manager have many clients with million-dollar accounts. They probably glance at yours once a month, if you are lucky. Fund managers make their money when the big dogs do, plain and simple.

A 401(k), while popular, is only one of three basic investment account options, and as a reminder, it is a retirement savings account offered by employers only. Individuals cannot invest in a 401(k) unless it is through an employer. Here are a few more investment options with explanations. If you get slightly confused, that's OK; we hope it will lead you to further your education and develop your investment skills. After you read the following you should get a sense of what investment options you are interested in. Continue to do your research because we will just be scratching the surface of each investment option. Knowing what type of investment interests you will help guide your continued exploration and eventual action in the investing game.

Investment Account #2 – IRA (Individual Retirement Account)

IRAs are just that...they are investment retirement accounts and nothing more. It is simply another "house" with its own "house rules" in which you can invest and grow your money. Now, to really make your head explode, there are variations on this type of account that we will briefly explore. We are only going to examine two of the four that are out there because they are the most popular and most likely to cross your investing paths.

First IRA Variation – Traditional IRA

Traditional IRA Definition: An individual retirement account (IRA) that allows individuals to direct pre-tax income, up to specific annual limits, toward investments that can grow tax-deferred (no capital gains or dividend income is taxed). Individual taxpayers are allowed to contribute 100 percent of compensation up to a specified maximum dollar amount to their traditional IRAs. Contributions to the traditional IRA may be tax-deductible depending on the taxpayer's income, tax-filing status and other factors.

This is a commonly known type of investment account (house). You put your money in tax-free, choose what specific stocks, bonds, or mutual funds, etc. (rooms in the house) you would like your money invested in, then upon withdrawal you pay taxes on the amount as ordinary income at the applicable tax rate. These, and all other types of accounts, are set up through banks or companies like Fidelity, Charles Schwab, MassMutual, Prudential, and Northwestern Mutual. There are specific "house rules" to this type of account such as minimum/maximum contributions based on your income, and when you are allowed access to your money without paying any penalties.

(Note: currently 401(k) and traditional IRA withdrawals are taxed at your income tax rate at the time of withdrawal. So if you wait until you are retired it is likely your tax rate will be lower as income is typically lower upon retirement. If you withdraw money before then it will be taxed at your current income tax bracket. The IRA variation below offers a very valid option to avoiding potentially paying higher taxes upon withdrawing your money.)

Second IRA Variation – Roth IRA

Roth IRA Definition: An individual retirement plan that has many similarities to the traditional IRA. However, contributions are *not* tax-deductible when you make them, and *withdrawals are tax-free*. Similar to other retirement plan accounts, non-qualified (read: rule-breaking) withdrawals from a Roth IRA may be subject to a penalty.

What this means is that contributions to your Roth IRA are made with post-tax dollars, i.e., your net income. Since Uncle Sam already got his cut you are allowed to allocate your money to this fund (with restrictions based on Roth IRA "house rules"), let it grow over time, and then withdraw that money tax-free when you've reached the qualifying age or meet other fund withdrawal criteria.

Our opinion: Mathematically, it makes more sense to invest in a Roth IRA if you meet the income qualifications. Better to pay income taxes before you make your investment, grow your money, and then take it out tax-free when permitted by your Roth IRA "house rules." There are different ways of making this investment as well. You can take $400 each month and invest it, or you can wait until December 15 and put in the maximum amount allowed for that year, which is currently $5,500 if you are under fifty years old, or $6,500 if you are over fifty (these amounts are set by the IRS).

Why might a Roth IRA be better than a traditional IRA? As an artist, you can actually take advantage of your "hard times" when you are not working as much. You are likely to meet the income limits Roth IRAs have that allow you to contribute. As your Thriving Artist growth continues, and your income streams grow exponentially, you will likely exceed the income limit and Roth IRAs will no longer be available to you. If you are just starting out in the investment game, Roth IRAs are a great place to begin.

Investment Account #3 – Taxable Brokerage Account

A taxable brokerage account is an investment account you can set up as an individual and do whatever you want with the money in that account. You can buy/sell any number of financial products (stocks, bonds, mutual funds, CDs, etc.), and you will pay applicable taxes on any gains you have from selling that product. There are no restrictions on how much money you can add to your account, no limits on the kind of investments you can make, and there are no required withdrawals or restrictions on withdrawals as with some other accounts we previously mentioned. Essentially this is an account (house) in which you can fill up the rooms with whatever financial products you like, and as much as you like. Again, see each investment account's "house rules" for details, but a taxable brokerage account allows you a bit more freedom; however, the tax implications are different and typically you will not be able to defer your taxes to a later date.

Joe: This is the type of account that I have with Fidelity.com. My very smart parents set me up with a brokerage account when I was in high school. I didn't have much to do with it then, but now I am in full control of the money and what it is invested in within that account. It has done wonders for my financial intelligence and learning about the game of investing. As of now it is still in there and doing well, but I keep a very close eye on it and should I see an opportunity or financial product that interests me, I am fully empowered to move that money where I see fit. I can also sell off all or part of the account for a down payment on a home or other large purchase… whatever the case may be, I'm in the driver's seat and it's a very good feeling.

With all of the investment accounts (houses) described above, here are some examples of the different types of specific investments (rooms) you can have in those accounts. Most brokerage houses have access to nearly all of what we describe below, however, some specialize in one type of investment over another. See what interests you here and then explore the different brokers who offer these types of financial products and investments.

Investment Option #1: Individual Stocks/Securities

You can buy and sell shares of any individual company that is listed on the New York Stock Exchange (NYSE), the Dow Jones Industrial Average (DJIA), NASDAQ, or almost any market in the world for that matter, thanks to online trading. A lot of artists are getting into this as a way of making extra money, and it is a great way to do it. It does require more time and research, but if you like doing your homework and picking a winning stock, this could be for you.

Joe: I use TD Ameritrade for my trades, but there are lots of other brokerage houses out there like E*Trade, Fidelity, Scottrade, and ShareBuilder. Also, each company may offer classes and tools to educate you as you get more advanced in your trades. Make sure you do a lot of research when you go "hands-on" like this. You can make a lot, but you can lose a lot too. Virtually all brokerage houses offer a service wherein you create an account and make "paper" or fake money trades so you can practice. Start yourself out with $50,000 of fake money and see how you do! Then when you are ready, you can deposit some real money (nothing more than you are comfortable with) and do it for real. Nothing changes the game more than when you have your money invested in a stock. You may have only purchased three shares of a company at $20 each, but that makes all the difference in the world. I highly recommend doing something like this, because it puts you on the playing field of investing in a big way.

Investment Option #2: Mutual Funds

Mutual funds are essentially groups of stocks that are picked to be in one "fund." Some funds are more aggressive and have higher gain/loss potential, and there are others that are more "safe" with a lower gain/loss potential. You can choose the type of fund you want your money to be in, but you cannot allocate your investment into one single stock like Apple or Starbucks. There are over a hundred investment companies out there to work with, such as Charles Schwab, T. Rowe Price, MassMutual, Prudential, and Fidelity just to name a few.

Mutual funds can be tricky. Can they make money? Sure. Can they lose money? Absolutely. If this is the investing route you are going to take, then as always do your research. Different companies have different funds and some are better than others. When you set up a mutual fund you will be assigned an account advisor. Like all advisors, he has many clients and his job is to get you to buy (invest in) mutual funds or other products from *his* company. We don't begrudge him for it, that is his job and he has to make a living, too. But, if he is really pushy or tells you that you have to get into this fund today "or else," then you need to find a different advisor. Never work with someone who is giving you an ultimatum. *Do not* feel pressured into any fund or company. Take your time and make a well-informed decision.

Investment Option #3: ETF (Exchange-Traded Fund)

An ETF is like a mutual fund in that it is a collection of stocks, but unlike a mutual fund you are able to buy and sell ETFs quickly throughout the trading day. They are essentially a group of stocks that trade like a single stock on the market, so you can purchase an ETF in the morning and then sell it a few hours later. Mutual funds have limits on how often you can buy/sell them and they always settle at the end of the trading day. So if you purchase a mutual fund at 10 a.m., you won't get it at the 10 a.m. price; you will get it at whatever price it is at by the close of the day (4 p.m. EST). ETFs allow you to take advantage of a hot trend in the marketplace by giving you access to several stocks through the purchase of only one ETF. If you see that technology is on the uptick you can purchase shares of a technology heavy ETF. That tech ETF may have holdings in Apple, Dell, Microsoft, Cisco, Equinix, Hewlett-Packard, and Gateway, but you only had to buy one ETF, and you are able to benefit from the gains of whatever stocks that ETF holds. Make sense?

Investment Option #4: Bonds

A bond is a debt security, similar to an I.O.U. When you purchase a bond, you are lending money to a government, municipality, corporation, federal agency, or other entity known as an issuer. An issuer can be any legal entity that develops, registers, and sells securities to finance its own operations.

In return for your money, the issuer provides you with a bond, in which it promises to pay a specified rate of interest during the life of the bond and to repay the face value of the bond (the principal) when it matures, or comes due.

Among the types of bonds available for investment are: U.S. government securities, municipal bonds, corporate bonds, mortgage- and asset-backed securities, federal agency securities, and foreign government bonds. All bonds have different characteristics, so do your research before investing in any specific type of bond.

For those with a lower risk tolerance, bonds may be an attractive investment because of their fixed interest rate that guarantees a return on the investment over time.

Investment Option #5: CDs

A Certificate of Deposit, or CD, is exactly what it sounds like. It is a certificate usually issued by a commercial bank to someone depositing money for a specified length of time (anywhere from one month to five years) at a fixed interest rate. As an incentive, banks offer an interest rate to the investor that is higher than a checking or savings account. CDs are lower-risk, lower-return investments, and are also known as "time deposits." There are strategies that one can use when investing in CDs, but the thing to remember is that you don't have access to this money. Even if you must absolutely get to it, you could face a tax penalty for taking it out early.

Most CDs that have higher percentage rates (i.e., pay more) are going to require you to invest your money for a minimum of two years. If you don't think you will need that money and you want to play it super safe, this might be a good option for you. Be aware that you may be able to negotiate your interest rate with the bank issuing you the CD. Remember, you are giving *them* money to work with and for that you should have some say in the rate you get in return. Obviously the larger your investment the more negotiating power you have. Always ask. The worst answer you'll get is no. Nothing ventured, nothing gained, right?

Investment Option #6: Annuities

An annuity is a contract between a financial institution and an annuity owner (you). In exchange for a purchase payment, or series of payments, the financial institution guarantees to pay a stream of income in the future. Annuities are primarily used as a means of securing a steady cash flow during one's retirement years. Keep in mind that the guarantees are based on the ability of the issuing company to pay the claim.

Investment Option #7: Commodities

Commodities are physical substances, such as metals (silver, gold, platinum), or food (grains, beef), which are interchangeable with another product, usually of the same type. The price of the commodity is subject to supply and demand. Investors most often buy or sell these commodities through futures contracts. A futures contract is a contractual agreement, generally made on the trading floor of a futures exchange, to buy or sell a particular commodity in the future at a price determined now. Some futures contracts may call for physical delivery of the asset, while others are settled in cash.

When people think of tradable commodities most often they think of silver, gold, platinum, corn, oil, or wheat. Historically, when the stock market is down, commodities are up (though that hasn't always been the case lately). For ease we will just talk about the two most popular metals, gold and silver: however, there are other metals and commodities out there to invest in. You can purchase and hold the physical metal if you wish, or you can look into several different gold or silver ETFs out there and just own "shares" of that commodity type.

Joe: I purchased some gold coins a while ago and I am glad I did. I like them because gold coins will always have value, whereas our currency may not. Since 1971, when we were taken off the gold standard – meaning all US money until that year was backed by physical gold in the Treasury – our currency has continued to lose value because there is no physical gold/silver to back it. So, in some ways gold is a safe haven in troubled economic times because its value tends to rise. Gold is a tangible investment; much like real estate, you can actually put your hands on it, but like any investment there is no guaranteeing that the price or value will increase.

Physical gold, silver, and other metals can be purchased through brokers such as Blanchard, Goldline, and Monex Precious Metals, to name a few. If you are interested in owning commodities "on paper," nearly all brokerage houses have access to ETFs in gold, silver, platinum, oil, wheat, etc. Pros and cons of both investment avenues can be argued, however, we will not go into them here. Suffice to say that, once again, you always need to do your research before choosing any investment.

Investment Option #8: Real Estate

Is it the Mecca of all investing? Some people say yes, some people say no. After the real estate mortgage meltdown of 2008 it seems nothing is certain, and those who thought they would never lose in the real estate game did in fact lose quite a bit. Even as we write this in a tough economic climate some people are making money on real estate, while many other people are in foreclosure and have lost their homes. The point we are making here is that *every investment has an element of risk!*

We have been saying all along to do your due diligence before you invest in anything, but *especially* do your homework before investing in real estate! Buying one or two gold coins probably won't bankrupt you if they go down in value, but buying an investment property in the wrong area, or not knowing that the home you are purchasing is infested with termites, could be the decision you regret for a long, long time.

Joe: A friend of mine whom I have done several shows with has really won at the real estate game. While he was on a Broadway national tour that was sitting down in LA for several months, he decided to invest in some real estate in town. Not long after he did so, the city rezoned his neighborhood and the value of his investment skyrocketed overnight! After refinancing and pulling a great deal of equity out of one property, he took that money and purchased other buildings, and his tenants pay his mortgages and then some. My friend has an incredibly sharp business mind and is a true example of a Thriving Artist who has created, and continues to create, several streams of income while still performing on Broadway and around the country.

Investment Option #9: REITs

REIT is an acronym for Real Estate Investment Trust. A REIT is an investment trust that owns and manages a pool of commercial properties, mortgages, and other real estate assets. It is an investment option that sells like a stock on the major exchanges and invests in real estate directly, either through properties or mortgages. REITs receive special tax considerations, and potentially offer investors high yields, as well as a highly liquid method of investing in real estate.

If you don't want to do the legwork of finding a property, checking it out, doing the research on the area, and then working to rent or sell it, you can let these guys do the work for you. REITs were extremely popular in the years leading up to the real estate bubble bursting in 2008 because you could get in on the hottest sectors in the country but not have to be an expert. A word of caution, however, because those who invested blindly got burned when the house of cards fell. No matter what, there is no such thing as a sure thing.

The game (yes, we see it as a game) of investing and growing your money can be one that is a lot of fun, or it can cause massive amounts of stress in your life. Most of the stress people feel is being overwhelmed, scared, and/or uneducated. We are here to make sure that is not the case for you. If you weren't previously aware of the above investment options, now you are. If you don't know anything about any of them, that is fine. Now you have some homework to do. *Please* do not just put your head in the sand because it all seems to be "too much to learn," or you are hoping someone else will take care of it for you. The talent of growing your money is one you will develop for the rest of your life…the sooner you start, the better!

(Note: if you feel sick to your stomach or completely overwhelmed at this point, please stop reading for a moment. Put this down and come back later. Go back and read this section on growing your money again and again until it makes sense. Only when you can read all of the above without panic or utter confusion should you move on.)

Now let us continue with the other Money Mastery Talents that you need in order to be a Thriving Artist.

MASTERY #5. CONTROL: All the Thriving Artists we know have a very good pulse on where their money is, how much they have, and what it is doing. When they need to move it, they have access and know exactly what to do, or consult with the right people beforehand. They have the keys to controlling every aspect of their finances.

If you have made some investments and perhaps they aren't going the way you planned, or you don't have a good feeling about them, there is nothing that says you have to stick with that investment, fund, or company. Why stay aboard a sinking ship? Again, do your research before taking action. Call your financial advisor. Pick up the *Wall Street Journal* or *Investor's Business Daily*. There is also an incredible amount of information online. Investing is like riding a roller coaster; there are twists and turns and ups and downs. If you start to feel like a particular roller coaster is too fast for you, you can always hop off and ride something else. The point is that you are investing *your* money, in *your* future, and it is *your* prerogative to invest that money as you see fit. You are in complete control.

Christine: As you can see, the point of looking after your own money and doing your due diligence keeps coming up. When the market crashed in 2008 a lot of people lost a lot of money. Joe had been doing a ton of reading and watching the stock market. He sensed a major downturn was coming. He proceeded to move most of our money into guaranteed funds; this included our 401(k), mutual funds, and the like. For this reason, when the market dropped several thousand points, we didn't take the ride down with it. I'm not saying that to boast: it is simply to illustrate the point that we were paying attention to what was happening and had the access and the know-how so we could act. We want the same for each of you reading this right now.

We can't tell you how many people say, "Oh, but it will come back." However, in terms of numbers, the "it will come back" looks like this: If you had $100,000 invested in mutual funds, you lost 20 percent ($20,000) when the stock market plummeted. Now you have $80,000 in your account. Let's say it takes the market two years to recover and your mutual fund has now gained 20 percent. *That does not mean that you are back to even.* You made back 20 percent of $80,000, not 20 percent of $100,000. Here is the math:

20 percent of $80,000 is $16,000

20 percent of $100,000 is $20,000

If your mutual funds earned back 20 percent, your balance is $96,000 and you aren't back to your original $100,000 yet. If you had moved your money before the crash and still had $100,000 and then caught just some of the recovery and earned 10 percent on your $100,000, your account would now have $110,000. That's a $14,000 difference. Of course, nobody knows exactly when things are going to happen and some financial "experts" will tell you that "timing the market" as we have just spoken about is not a good idea. We were right this time because we were actively in the game, and *that* is the point we are driving at for you.

In addition to knowing where and when to move money that you have invested, we also want to share with you a few systems for controlling every penny you make. The percentages you are about to see are not important, but the discipline of controlling where your money goes as soon as you make it is extremely important.

The very simplest way of controlling your active or passive income (money that comes to you from a job or some form of residual asset that pays you on a regular basis) is using the 50/50 system. It breaks down like this:

> **50 percent** you spend on whatever you need to: food, clothing, rent/ mortgage, toys, gadgets, entertainment, etc. You essentially live off of this money.

50 percent you save. You put the money in the bank and/or your investment money comes from this as well. You can do what you like with this money; you just have to save it in some form or another.

A more advanced way of managing your income is the 70/10/10/10 system. How that breaks down is this:

70 percent is for living expenses, bills, food, and entertainment.
10 percent you save.
10 percent you invest.
10 percent you give to charity.

The next level above that is the 50/10/10/10/10/10 system (as seen in T. Harv Eker's book *Secrets of the Millionaire Mind.* That breaks down as follows:

50 percent is for living expenses
10 percent you save and never touch (only spend the interest that it generates)
10 percent you save for large purchases (car, house, boat)
10 percent you use for education (financial education/classes/books)
10 percent you give away
10 percent you spend on *yourself* in whatever way makes you feel good

We use this third system and it has proven to be very effective. It completely eliminates the question "Do I have money for that?" Every time you earn a check you divide it into these categories and then when you need it, it will be there for you. You can have several bank accounts to actually move the money into, or you can keep track on a sheet of paper. Whatever works, *and that you know you will stick with*, do it.

The last thing we do to control our money is to calculate our net worth at the beginning of every month. We do this like clockwork, because as we stated at the beginning of this book, "Everything is energy and what you focus on increases" and since we focus on our financial well-being, it tends to get better and better all the time. Go to our website and download our Thriving Artists Net Worth Tracking Sheet, so you can have a guide when you start doing it for yourself. In short, you simply add up all your assets, money in the bank, money invested, current stock values, and you subtract all outstanding debts that you have such as a mortgage, credit card debt, car loan etc. The number you come out with is your current net worth. It is a very good wake-up call if you see a number that is lower than you expected, or it can be a wonderful validation that you are doing things right if you see it going up month after month. The practice of holding the mirror up to your financial face on a regular basis is a sacred one. How else are you going to spot those blemishes and correct them? Or how else are you going to see just how beautiful you really are?

As you can already tell, we cannot urge you strongly enough to get (or stay) in the driver's seat and control your money. Paying attention and taking an active role in your investments and money management will separate you from the pack of starving artists, and you will be well on your way to a Thriving future!

MASTERY #6. GIVE: You get what you give in this world…we believe that whole-heartedly. Every single one of us has something to give, no matter how small the amount. We have come across people, seminars, and books that tell you that you *must* give away a certain amount or percentage of your income. If that works for you and you feel good doing it then by all means continue to do so. We are not here to make judgments in any way, only to share our philosophy and what has worked for us in our experience.

We believe that you should give away only what you feel good about giving away. If that is not the case with you and you do not feel good about what you've given, then whatever you did give isn't as good a gift as it could be — it hints of an obligation. Obligations can lead to resentment if one is not careful, and that is not the feeling *we* want to have, nor do we want *you* to have when you are giving. The saying "Everything is energy" really holds true here. If you are giving happily and freely and you are not feeling any sense of loss from your gift, then the amplification of that act — the good karma, if you will — gets released into the Universe. We all know the adage of "What goes around comes around," right? So make sure that what "goes around" is pure and carries a great intention and energy with it.

MASTERY #7. PROTECT: Protecting your money is something that you have to worry about more when you are making a lot of it, but it is never too early to learn about this topic. There are several ways to protect what you earn. For example, you can form a corporation and filter your money/income through it. The implications of doing this can be complex, but in essence you turn yourself into an LLC, an S-Corp, or C-Corp (look them up) and when you get a job, the employer does not hire *you*, they hire your corporation, and then your corporation pays you a salary. Please keep in mind that there are benefits and drawbacks to doing this depending on how much you are making. You should definitely direct this question to a CPA (Certified Public Accountant) and/or a CFP (Certified Financial Planner) before taking any action in this area. It is highlighted here because down the line it can become very important that you protect yourself and what you earn.

OK, pause. We put a lot of information into this section to provide a sampling of what you should know to make your finances work in this lifelong career. Take a moment to go back over all the Thriving Artists Money Mastery Talents and make sure you understand everything. We still have more information to share about finances and investing, so when you feel ready, continue on.

Chapter 9 – Real-World Advice
Some Life Lessons about Money, Investing, and Owning a Home

The School of Life is one that you are always enrolled in whether you like it or not. You can try to skip class, and of course there are times when all of us want to, but class is *always* in session. It is patiently waiting for you to come back in and sit down for another lesson. But more often than not we learn the information we needed just *after* we needed it! Life has an ironic sense of humor that way don't you think? We generally call what we learn "experience." But, since you are just one person and can't experience everything, here are some of the financial lessons we have learned along the way. Sometimes it takes a village…

Lesson #1 – Questioning the "You must buy an apartment!" advice

How many times have you heard, "Oh, once you are on Broadway, you *must* buy an apartment!"? We have been asked if we own an apartment/house countless times. Do we own yet? No. Do we want to own a home? Yes, when the time is right. Granted, we were looking in one of the most expensive markets in the country. If we lived in our hometown of Harrisburg, PA we could absolutely buy a home. The game is a little different in NYC and LA.

Still, so many people kept telling us we just *had* to buy an apartment. So we thought, "OK, maybe there's something to that," and we started looking. At that time the price of a two-bedroom apartment in Astoria, New York (Queens) was around $550,000 for about 700–900 square feet. We weren't even looking in Manhattan, and prices were *that* high in an outer borough. We needed a two-bedroom because we knew we wanted to have a family within a few years and a one-bedroom just didn't make any sense.

The math of a $550,000 mortgage on an apartment is about $3,000 a month. Our estimates were always for a 30-year, fixed rate of about 6.5 to 7 % with 10–15 percent down. Luckily, many of the new apartments in Astoria had tax abatements — a reduction of <u>taxes</u> or an <u>exemption</u> from taxes granted by a <u>local</u> government—on them, so tax figures were extremely low. (As of this writing the interest rates are much lower, so you can adjust the numbers accordingly. We simply want to give a real-life example of what we went through.)

There were also common charges that ranged from $300 to $600 a month depending on the size of the apartment. This is before we would buy one bit of food or a MetroCard to get to work each day. Could we afford that mortgage? Yes, if both of us were on Broadway, or if one of us was on Broadway and the other had a steady income stream from another source. But we would really have needed to tighten our belts on *everything* else. It also might have tied one of us into a less-than-ideal survival job and not allowed us the time freedom we wanted. We know that we just wrote about creating income from a source that you love, but if you give yourself a huge monthly mortgage, it can change the landscape entirely. To us that was unacceptable. We both refused to be hostages to our home and still do.

Christine: Joe never wanted to feel pressured into continuing with Hairspray *any longer than he felt comfortable. I wouldn't want that either. Some of you may think that's crazy. Why wouldn't you stay in your Broadway show? Joe did. He did the tour for nearly two years and the Broadway for over two and a half years. It was time to move on. We both believe in the power of energy and intention and if you're not careful you can get stuck.* Hairspray *was an amazing show and an amazing job, but there comes a time when you need to spread your wings again. We had the flexibility to do that. If we had bought that apartment, he would have been forced to be a "Nicest Kid in Town" for as long as the show ran. There is nothing wrong with doing that, but for us it would not have been our idea of living the life of a Thriving Artist (inspiration, empowerment, and entrepreneurship).*

We both believe that being artists and getting to perform is the best job you can have. But here's the rub; it is still a *job*, and jobs come and go. The key question you *must* ask yourself before you sign on the dotted line for that mortgage is: "Can I afford this property whether I am in a show or not, and how long can I afford to carry this mortgage if my show closes and I am in between jobs?" This is a crucial question to answer! There is no "get out of jail free" card. The bank doesn't care that *Ragtime* closed too soon or the financing for your commissioned symphony fell through. Please proceed with extreme awareness.

We also chose not to give up the lifestyle that we had grown accustomed to. We enjoyed seeing shows, going out to eat and taking vacations when we wanted. We were not about to go back on ramen noodles and Chinese food so we could afford our apartment. It just wasn't worth it. After we discovered that a two-bedroom was not in the cards yet, we started looking at a one-bedroom. Why? Because everyone kept saying, "*You have to buy an apartment!*" Eventually we did find a one-bedroom apartment in Astoria for $369,000. Our mortgage would have been about $1800 a month, certainly more doable; unfortunately, we would have needed to get rid of a lot of our furniture. We were in a two-bedroom at the time and would need to downsize to fit into the smaller space. Did this make sense? It didn't make sense to us either, but *we had to buy an apartment.* So we continued down the rabbit hole…

The realtor advised us to put in an offer of $350,000, which we did. Our offer was rejected and we took that as a sign and we stopped looking. Shortly after that we spoke with our good friend and real estate guru, Sue Gilad. She enlightened us a bit by pointing out a few things. Why were we upping our expenses when we didn't have to? We had very cheap rent where we were and did not need the extra room right now. Also, there wasn't a baby in the picture at the moment, and why would we up our monthly financial nut? "*Because we HAVE TO buy an apart-ment!*" we said. But, why? Again we said, "*BECAUSE WE HAVE TO BUY AN APARTMENT!*" She just smiled quietly, and we finally understood that *we* were creating the stress and the unnecessary urgency. So we stopped doing that and continued enjoying things just as they were, and in the meantime continued to build our other income streams.

What's funny is that we didn't even really like the apartment we had put the offer on. It's amazing how things work out isn't it?

Christine: A word of caution from our personal experience: When we were thinking about the $550,000 apartment, we met with a mortgage broker and a few banks. You wouldn't believe some of the things they offered. Among the many deals we were presented with to "get us in that apartment" was an interest-only mortgage. This means you pay only the interest and none of the principal for a set amount of time. So if we were borrowing $450,000 from the bank at 6.8 percent, our interest-only payment would be about $2,550. It would have taken us much longer to pay off our apartment, because we would be just paying the interest at first, and we still *would owe $450,000! My dad said something very wise: "If you need an interest-only loan, you can't afford it." He was absolutely right!*

Also, beware of adjustable-rate loans. They have their place and they do work for some people, but you really have to know what you are dealing with. You may be offered a mortgage at 3.5 percent for five years, but after that it adjusts to the current interest rate. In five years, interest rates could be 7 percent. That would double your interest payment, plus you are paying the principle of the loan on top of that. Yes, the rate could decrease giving you a lower monthly payment, but you have to ask yourself if you are willing to take that gamble? We have heard many people say, "Oh, you won't be in that apartment in five years. You'll sell it and buy a house before then." Well, we all know; "life" happens. What if five years from your purchase date was the winter when nobody could sell their property and foreclosures were at an all-time high? What if you lost your job? Or perhaps your apartment didn't appreciate as much as you had estimated? Chances are you cannot afford that new house now. Five years can go by very quickly and your financial situation may not have improved as much as you thought it would.

Here is the math on an interest-only adjustable-rate mortgage. You bought an apartment and needed to borrow $350,000 from the bank. You signed an adjustable-rate mortgage for 5 years. Your rate for the first five years is 3.5 percent. This makes your mortgage payment $1,020.83 per month. Let's say you are still in the same apartment five years later and your mortgage rate is going to adjust. Let's now make your interest rate 6.5 percent. Your mortgage payment is now $1,895.83. This is a difference of $875 per month! Will that be a problem? Who knows? Will you have the same job? If you get a raise, will it be enough? Do you plan to have kids in those first five years? With this bit of a reality check, how much do you love your apartment now?

So be *very* careful and don't get in over your head. A mortgage lender can be extremely persuasive. His job is to sell you a mortgage. Of course people *should* be ethical in their business dealings, but unfortunately that is not always the case. Ultimately, we believe the responsibility is on you. Don't cry when rate changes that were on the contract take effect that you didn't read the fine print. *Read it and understand it before you sign anything.*

There are free mortgage calculators available, so punch in your numbers and see what comes out. We both have an app on our phones and use it all the time. If you get a nauseated feeling in your stomach when you see the number, listen to your gut. Remember, this monthly mortgage payment is before you turn on a light, eat anything, or pump up the heat on a cold night.

There is nothing wrong with renting. Let us say that again. *There is nothing wrong with renting.* Buying a home can be much like joining a union. You have to make sure you are ready. When buying a home, you should have a good/excited feeling in your stomach. Of course you are going to be a little nervous, but it should be similar to the sensation you had when you chose a college, made your move to either coast, or on your wedding day! You are nervous, but you know that what's ahead will be great. If you can't sleep at night and you wonder how you are going to afford it if there is just one misstep, it may not be the right time yet.

Sometimes we feel like the parents who have to tell their kids no. You may want an apartment, or a new car, but you can't have it right now. Don't try to keep up with the Joneses. You haven't seen their bank account. They may be up to their ears in debt while they drive their fancy cars and have the latest gadgets.

Lesson #2 - Winning the renters' game

Since we just talked about buying, let us now talk about renting. A huge pitfall that young artists (specifically performers) succumb to is the "gotta live in midtown" (or some other trendy neighborhood) mentality. They might live in an outer borough for a while, but only long enough to find their "perfect" apartment in Manhattan. We touched on this before, but it's worth repeating. Do not become one of the "Young, Fabulous, On Broadway, and *Broke*" crowd. If you have a good place in Queens, Brooklyn, the Bronx, or Jersey that is cheap and you catch that dream Broadway contract, *please do not pack up and move to midtown just because you can*! Chances are you're going to up your rent by around 50 percent or more, and you are putting all of your eggs in one basket by hoping that your show will run a long time. We heard this story directly from someone who did just what we described, and they were stressed out like crazy. They had no money after their move to midtown and the show quickly thereafter got its closing notice.

If you have other income sources, *if* you find a killer deal in a good/safe location in the hottest neighborhood, then by all means go if you like. But *don't go* just because you feel like you need to be "seen on the scene." It's a colossal waste of money. People will take the train or the jitney to your game night.

Lesson #3 - Beware the "Buy now, pay later" mentality

Have you ever thought, "I will put this purchase (whatever you feel you must have) on my credit card and just keep transferring it until I have the money to pay it off." We are sorry to tell you, but *you can't afford it.* Exercise a little restraint. Many people (us included) never carry a balance on their credit cards that cannot be paid off in full the next month. If we think we can't completely pay it off, we don't buy it. We are not mentioning that to gloat or brag: we mention it because it has kept us on a very good financial track and we hope you are on one (or get yourself on one) as well! So once again the answer is, "No, you can't have it right now." We don't care what everyone else does; make do with what you have. Sorry if we sound like your parents, but know it is out of love that we hit you over the head.

> (Note: This "can't put it on your credit card" mentality does not apply to medical emergencies or family situations that are uncontrollable and unexpected. Life happens and you never know what is lurking around the bend. Sometimes you have to put a trip home or a medical bill on your credit card and take some time to pay it off. We hope that with your new financial knowledge, you won't ever have to do that because you will have the money saved.)

But, we aren't just going to sit here and wag a finger at you. Our mission is to inspire and empower you. So let's now turn your "I can't afford it" into an *action-inducing* question of *"How can I* afford it?" Ask this question for anything you want that would make you carry a balance on your credit card. Asking, "How can I?" immediately takes you out of a static place of sitting there wanting something, and catapults your brain into thinking of solutions that require you to take action. You *can* have anything you want…you just have to figure out a responsible way to get it.

Continue down your path of financial education and skill building, and you will have enough income and/or cash savings to cover those unforeseen circumstances. That is a powerful shift to make. Knowing you can take whatever life throws at you, puts you in a whole new frame of mind… and once you can do that you are one step further on your journey of success!

Lesson #4 - Take your investment blinders off

Joe: (This story bears repeating so stick with us.) Investment blinders are a huge no-no. In the late fall of 2007, the world recession started creeping around the financial world. I very quickly took our 401(k), mutual funds, and anything else that was heavily invested in the stock market, and moved it mostly into guaranteed accounts. What does this mean? I put them in an account where they earned a guaranteed fixed rate of 3 percent no matter what the market did. We wouldn't cash in on any market surges, but we wouldn't take the ride down with the Titanic either. With all the news at that time, I was not willing to take that chance and wanted to protect our investments. I am not mentioning this to boast. I'm only adding it here as an example of what you can do to protect and grow your money, by paying attention to what is happening in the market and around the financial world. Throwing your money into some fund with some manager and hoping that something good comes of it is surely not the smart thing to do.

Let's be honest, we don't have a crystal ball and we aren't acting like we do. We paid attention and made what turned out to be a good move. Not everything we have done with our investments has panned out as well. The point we are making is that you have to be aware of your investments at all times, and you cannot manage those investments by simply hoping that someone else will do it for you.

Lesson #5 - Financial rules; Make them and follow them

You are an artist and that means that you can sing, dance, act, paint, direct, compose or all of the above, extremely well. What about the skills we should have, but perhaps didn't, learn in school? Skills like balancing our checkbooks or reading a financial statement, knowing the difference between a 401(k) and Roth IRA. Were we taught how to create a budget and stick to it? These are skills you that can literally take to the bank. Find different classes, systems, and mentors and learn everything you can. Take what works for you from all that you learn, create your own financial rules, and then follow them!

These are some financial golden rules we have learned over the years that we would like to pass on to you now.

We call them "**The Thriving Artists Ten Commandments**":

1. Thou shalt not live beyond thy means.

2. Thou shall only spend a maximum of two weeks' pay on thy dwelling.

3. Thou shalt not carry credit card balances.

4. Keep holy Tax Day, April 15.

5. Honor payment due dates and plan accordingly.

6. Thou shalt never get an interest-only mortgage (without doing your homework).

7. Thou shalt not live off thy savings & unemployment unless there is a family or medical emergency.

8. Thou shalt not try to fool or trick the IRS.

9. Thou shalt not covet thy neighbors' iPad, apartment, car, or gadget and try to conform financially (aka "keeping up with the Joneses").

10. Thou shalt come off all tours with more money than before thou left.

Lesson #6 - Thriving finances on tour and out of town

Between the two of us, by December 2011 we had worked at more than thirteen top regional theatres across the country and ten national and international tours. Sometimes our regional theatre jobs lasted two weeks and sometimes over two months. As for our touring lives, we were on the road with all our shows for a minimum of six months and one as long as nearly two years. Both of us really enjoy working out of town, particularly on tour. You get to live in a hotel, you don't really have to cook, and other than remembering to pay your cell phone bill on time and not missing your cast bus to the airport, there isn't a whole lot to worry about.

Christine: In fact, I sometimes had a hard time adjusting to life back in NYC after being on tour. I had to clean my apartment, I was auditioning again, and those pay checks weren't being direct deposited into my account every Thursday. What I didn't have a hard time adjusting to, though, is the amount of money we had saved from our various tours, or when I paid off my school loan while on the road with The Best Little Whorehouse in Texas.

There are a number of reasons to go on tour. See if any of these sound familiar or appealing to you:

1. It's a job!

2. It's a role or show that you have been dying to do.

3. It would be great to have that director/choreographer's name on your resume.

4. The Broadway show is still running and it's a possible way to ride that wave all the way to Broadway.

5. If you can sublet your apartment or move your stuff into storage, you can make a big dent in your debt or wipe it out completely (if you have any).

6. You can save up for a down payment on an apartment/house.

7. You hate summers and/or winters in New York City and an eight-week stop in LA sounds heavenly.

8. You need weeks for your insurance and/or you want to invest more in your 401(k).

9. You just broke up with your significant other and being in New York sounds like hell to you right now.

All of these are good reasons for going on tour, although if number 9 applies to you, we're sorry! Maybe a tour or a "show-mance" is just what the doctor ordered.

If your reasons for going on the road are artistic, great! Of course we want all artists to work as much as possible. If numbers 5, 6, and 8 sound appealing, we like where your head is financially! Before the tiered touring contracts* were created, production contracts* were not all that rare. Nowadays, we can almost count on one hand how many full production contracts are currently on tour. That is sobering. Why? If you can sublet your place, or significantly decrease your expenses in your home city while on the road, you can save a *ton* of money on the full production contract. Now, don't misunderstand, we have both done a tiered touring contract and saved money. It can be done. For actors, it *must* be done; otherwise you are going to find yourself trying to climb the mountain to financial freedom for a long time. There may be some sacrifices that you have to make for a few months or a year, but aren't those worth peace of mind financially? We are going to be tough here. We have (unfortunately) seen a whole lot of people come off the road with no money saved or worse—they come back with less than when they packed their trunk to leave. We cannot stress enough; the money decisions you make (or don't make now) will affect you in the future. Either way, you cannot get that time or money back. You may think, "Oh, I'll get another tour and I'll save then, but for now I'm going to live it up!" We hope for your sake, that you are right and you do book lots of jobs, but nothing is for sure in this world and we have to be disciplined when we have a great paying gig.

>*Tiered touring contract: A few years ago when a lot of first national tours were going out non-union, the League of Producers and Equity came up with new tiered touring contracts. This enabled a show to go out union, yet be allowed to pay the actors less than full production contract scale. These were specifically designed for "soft" hits, i.e., shows that weren't blockbusters like *Wicked* or *Jersey Boys*. We won't go into all of the specifics of this contract here. Go to www.actorsequity. org if you would like more information.

>*Production contract: This is the highest-paid Actors Equity Association contract. This includes Broadway, and national tours. Your starting salary is the current production salary whether you are in New York or on the road. For national tours, these are your big hits, like the shows we mentioned above.

Christine: In August of 2010, I found myself sitting in a two-bedroom condo in Chicago. Joe had booked the first national tour of Shrek the Musical *and I had come along for the ride with our then eight-month-old boy, Cole. After* The Little Mermaid *closed, Joe had taken some time off and we got the apartment ready for our new arrival. When Cole was about six weeks old and we were starting to get the hang of the whole parenting thing, Joe started auditioning again. He had some great auditions and callbacks for regional theaters, but no long-term job offers. We were looking for another Broadway show or a big tour. Our priorities had changed now. Joe hated being away from Cole, even for a day or two. Lo and behold, the big green ogre called. Joe booked* Shrek the Musical *as a swing. He was covering eight ensemble men and with all of the extra parts/covers that entails, it seemed financially possible (remember, this is on a tiered contract). We weren't in our 20's anymore and if you remember at the beginning of this book, I mentioned being a Thriving Artist for your whole career. We had more bills and Cole wasn't bringing in any cash as a Gap baby just yet, so... to the road we went!*

After doing the math, we decided to give up our apartment, put our stuff in storage near family in Pennsylvania (saving $100/month in the process), and the three of us packed our bags. Our plan was to save as much money as we could—hence cutting as many expenses as possible—and then buy a home in New Jersey after tour. Well, as the saying goes, "If you want to make God laugh, tell Him your plans!" As we write this, it is April of 2013 and we are all settled here in Los Angeles. It is a far cry from owning a house in New Jersey and we will tell the story perhaps in the next edition of this book, but suffice to say, we were very disciplined with our Shrek tour money. It is what covered all of our expenses to move our lives out here from back east.

Luckily, we did save money on tour, because the pay was close to a full production contract. I almost choked on my tongue when I heard that the Young Frankenstein tour, after being a full production contract, would be going out on a whole new SETA (Short Engagement Touring Agreement) contract. The salaries were in the $700/week range and the per diem was around $42/day and you had to stay in the housing the company chose for you. As a contract for people just getting out of school that is a wonderful thing. I understand the economics of different touring markets and "in this economy", blah, blah, blah. But, Joe and I could not afford to do that job. That's not a complaint, just a mathematical fact of our lives.

The per diem on Shrek was $798 a week. The company gave us two options for housing or we were free to find our own. If the company housing was over $70/ night, the company would pick up the difference based on an average. Because we had choices on this contract, Joe and I actually saved a fair portion of our per diem in Chicago. The company housing, while great, came in at roughly $2,600/month ($650/week), which would leave $568/month ($142/week) to eat on. Now, because these were apartments with full kitchens, you could, of course, save money by eating at home most of the time. We are sure you are aware that it is very easy to spend $100 per week on groceries! That now leaves you with $168/month ($42/week) to see movies, go sightseeing, and so on. Joe and I did a little digging and found a place for $1,600/month. It was a sub-lease on an apartment with lots of amenities. We spent $1,600/month of the $3,168 total monthly per diem that we were given. That left us with $1,568/month or $392/week to live on. Are you catching on? Joe and I wanted to completely save his salary. So that meant that our cell phone bills, food, gas, and any other expenses had to be paid on that $1,568 we had left. If you are living in company housing, you are more than likely dipping into your salary to take *care of some bills and over time it can add up. Saving money like that didn't happen everywhere, but it was something we strived for in every city. This is just one example of how that can be done.*

Let's be honest here. If you are going to go on the road for a year or more, away from your friends and family and miss all those weddings and birthdays, shouldn't you come back with a *fat* bank account? We know of people who went on the original *Phantom of the Opera* tour for a few years and were able to come back and buy a home in NYC. It is much harder to do that on the new *Young Frankenstein* contract unless you buy in Smalltown, USA.

Joe: Back to our point about setting up a recurring stream of income: You have to have something else paying you consistently to make a long career in this business. It is just a fact you have to face because $700/week before taxes ain't gonna cut it when you are in your thirties and want to support your family. And believe us, your thirties show up a lot faster than you think they will, and I know the same can be said for your forties and fifties and beyond. At some point you are going to tire of being forced to live the "bohemian" life. It's great when you are young, but our wish is for you to have the freedom to do the work you want, when you want. Especially as you get older, ramen noodles just don't taste as good anymore.

So, how do you save money on tour other than looking for cheaper housing options?

Eat in: Even if it is just breakfast, you can save anywhere from $10–$20 a day by having some oatmeal, healthy cereal, or low-fat yogurt in your room. If you don't have a refrigerator, use the ice buckets, or carry a cooler (it doesn't have to be a big one).

Make coffee/tea in your room: Again, if you use milk/cream, keep it on ice or snag the little creamers from a diner. A coffee at Starbucks, Dunkin', or Cosi is going to run you at least $1.65 or more every time. And you will of course be tempted to have a scone or a muffin. Who wouldn't, right? So your $1.50 coffee just turned into a $5 "snack" and you didn't even try.

Buy some healthy food to keep in the room and you will have meals for days. The pennies add up. We are not saying you shouldn't go out and have a nice breakfast once in a while. We especially liked having a diner-style breakfast on a matinee day. It helped us to get moving and energized for two shows. A friend, who was on the *Whorehouse* tour with Christine ate a whole lot of Subway® while on tour. People would make fun of her for it, but she came home and bought an apartment. The people who made fun of her didn't buy a thing... because they couldn't.

> (Note: We are not saying to only eat Subway or other cheaper food from chain restaurants. We know you must eat well and maintain a healthy body while on the road. The point is, however, to be aware of nickel-and-diming yourself into the poorhouse when it comes to eating on tour.)

Take public transportation: We know how nice it is to take cabs. There are times when you absolutely *should* take a cab. If you are out at night and it's late, by all means, hail one. Be smart though and share with a fellow cast member. Save yourself $5 here and there.

But during the day, if you need to get somewhere that is beyond the realm of walking, check out the bus system. Most cities that you will tour through have pretty great public transportation systems. If you want to take a road trip on a day off, plan it with some other cast members and split the cost of the rental car.

One of the cast members on *Shrek* bought a bike on Craig's List for $40 for the ten weeks that the show was in Chicago. He rode that thing everywhere and at the end of the ten weeks, he sold it. Pretty smart. If your sit-down engagements are a month or longer, most cities have a transit "saver pass." In big cities like San Francisco, Philadelphia, Washington, D.C., tricks like this could prove very cost-effective.

Save on post-show booze: You don't have to sell either one of us on the merits of a post-show drink. We love it! Again, once or twice a week, go out and have a nice drink at the bar. However, if you like your glass of red after a show and want to save some coin, buy a bottle, invite some folks over, and have a night in. Have game night and booze it up if you like! You can get a pretty good bottle anywhere from $7.99–$15.99. You will pay at least $8–$12 for that same *glass* of wine at a bar.

Travel buyout strategy: On a lot of tours, if you opt out of taking the company flight, you will receive that money to get yourself to the next city (although check with your company manager as this is something that is not as common as it once was).

Christine: On My Fair Lady, *we were supposed to fly from Cincinnati to Milwaukee. That is not a typical flight path like New York to Chicago, so the flight was expensive, around $350. A few cast members and I looked into renting a minivan and driving it instead. The drive was about six hours. We rented the van for under $150 and only had to fill the tank twice. Our total expenses were about $200: split three ways it was $71.60 per person, thus saving us $279 each. It all adds up! Plus there was a casino in Milwaukee.*

The trend for tiered tours as of now (speaking from the *Shrek* tour experience) is that you will receive a travel buyout up to $200 or the price of the flight, whichever is lower. So you'll never get more than $200 per flight when you opt out. We always took the buyout on the *Shrek* tour, because we drove to every city. Sometimes we came out ahead, sometimes we broke even, and sometimes we went in the hole a bit if we had a two-day drive. Flight buyouts are on a tour-by-tour basis, because as of now we don't believe there is any language in our AEA (Actors' Equity Association) contract with the League of Producers that states we get whatever they would have spent on our travel. They (the producers) may argue it's an expense for them, but it's not, because that money is already in the budget to move the cast from point A to point B. So whenever possible, we say fight for the entire buyout, and talk to AEA representatives and have them work it into the next round of negotiations if they haven't already.

Take full advantage of frequent flier miles/hotel and rental car programs/ reward credit cards: One would think it goes without saying, *but join every frequent flyer program on every airline you fly*! Even though you aren't paying for the flight yourself, you can collect all of those thousands of miles you rack up as you travel. Join the Hilton Honors Program, Marriott Rewards and every other hotel program out there. There is never a charge for this, and again, you will start raking in the points. If you rack up enough rewards, you will start earning free nights. Also, when you are a member of these programs, they usually deliver newspapers right to your door, give you free coffee, and other fun perks. For some hotel programs, instead of using your points for free nights, you can put those points toward frequent flyer miles as well.

Christine: While on tour with Shrek *we were going to stay at many Marriott hotels, so Joe and I got a Marriott Rewards Visa credit card. We are not usually fans of cards that have an annual fee, but this one is free for the first year and then only $30 per year after that. This card is a little ridiculous (in a great way!). At the time we were approved for our card, we got about 22,000 points and three free nights just for registering! We got one point for every dollar we spent and three points per dollar spent when we used our Marriott Visa to pay for our stays at any Marriott property. We had a ton of points because we put all of our hotels on this card, and then completely paid it off each month. This was a great way to save more of our per diem! When our tour stopped for a week in Tampa, Florida and we stayed at a Marriott Residence Inn we had six nights for free! Not too shabby! One other important thing about the points is that usually they never expire, so you can rack them up and use them for an end-of-tour-vacation if you like. Rules change all the time for these types of cards so be sure to check the details.*

Gym memberships – find them, haggle for them, trade for them!

Christine: I had a really cheap nationwide membership to Bally's Total Fitness for about ten years. It came in handy when I was on tour, but it was only because my membership was so cheap, that I didn't want to lose it. Otherwise it's not really worth keeping a membership if you are heading out on tour. Sometimes your team of company managers can work out deals with a local gym by throwing some tickets their way. If they don't work out a free membership, they generally work out a lower monthly rate, or some sort of weekly discount, so you can get your time in pumping iron or taking classes. Some other free options are, taking a jog, doing workout DVDs in your room, carrying resistance bands to do your own workout at the theater, and so on. If you are a yogi, hit up the local yoga studios and see if you can work out a deal there. Most studios have some sort of offer for new students, where you can get unlimited classes for the week for only $20. Again, do a little research and see what you can come up with. It will be well worth it!

Joe: When I was on tour with Hairspray, *our company managers were not big gym goers so I took it upon myself to work out deals wherever I could. While we were in Chicago, I found the coolest gym I have ever been to (and I've been to quite a few), the Lakeshore Athletic Club. This was a gym with seven levels that were formed in a horseshoe around a 100-foot rock-climbing wall that went right down the middle of the structure. I luckily stumbled upon it because our company housing was right near there...a happy accident indeed. Long story short, I was able to work out a* *deal with the club sales manager and we only paid $97 for the nine weeks we were in town. Regular club fees ran in the $100–$175 per month range and we were getting in for less than $50! There is strength in numbers, so if you pool your cast and go to the sales manager with some "found money" to throw their way, they will always work with you. Also, it is a feather in their cap that they have the touring cast of XYZ Broadway Show working out at their gym. Get a signed poster for them and your stock goes up even more! We had a great time at that gym, and it is where I found my love of rock climbing that I still have to this day. So get in there and flex your negotiating muscles…you never know what you'll be able to work out, so you can work out!*

Get a roommate: This can be a touchy subject for some, but if done right will save you oodles of cash. Let's say your two options for hotels are $79/night for the Hyatt and $59/night for the Homewood Studio Suites. There are a few possible scenarios here.

1. You choose to stay alone at the cheaper hotel, the Homewood Studio Suites. For seven nights at $59/night you will spend $413 (and let's say that that includes taxes). These rooms have kitchens so you will probably spend about $100 on groceries for the week. In total you will spend about $513 of your per diem and save **$279** for that week.

2. You choose to stay alone at the Hyatt, which is $79/night. On some contracts like *Shrek the Musical* (Tier B) the company will pay any housing difference over $70. So you are roughly paying $70/night. For seven nights you will spend $490 of your per diem. Let's say you take our advice and eat a few breakfasts and lunches in, spending roughly $50 on groceries (since you are only using a cooler and/or ice bucket to store food) and then about $125 on eating out. (Note: A lot of hotels do have refrigerators and microwaves, and they are sometimes free and sometimes not.) In total you will spend about $665 of your per diem and save **$127** for that week.

3. You decide to room with someone at the Homewood Studio Suites, and now you are only paying $29.50 a night and thus spending $206.50 on housing for seven nights. You still spend $100 on groceries, which brings your weekly total to only $306.50. You save **$485** of your per diem for that week! Would that make a difference week after week?

You *are* catching on, right? Let's be conservative and say on average by rooming with someone in every city, you save **$250**/week of your per diem. If you stay with the show for a year, that's **$13,000**! Let us say that again. That's **$13,000** saved from your per diem. This is not including what you are saving from your salary. We hope that your jaw just dropped a little. That's some real coin.

OK, we get it. We all know that sometimes you need a week off to stay by yourself here and there. You are at the theatre with these people, hanging out with them after the show, riding the bus to the airport, and flying on the plane...all with the same group of people. Of course you need your own space. The Thriving Artists choice is to take those weeks when the hotel options are $55/night or less and bunk in with a pal. In the long run your bank account will thank you.

We know the big cities like San Francisco, Washington, D.C., Miami, and Boston are a lot more expensive, and even if you do room with someone, you may not be able to save $200–$300 of your weekly per diem. Fine. But ultimately, after a year tour, if you double up most of the time and factor in those expensive cities, you can still save roughly **$7,000–$8,000.** Not chump change by any means.

We have both done tours with people who say they absolutely cannot room with anyone. OK, but we don't want to hear one bit of complaining that you aren't saving any money. After you have been with the tour for a bit, you will find out whom you gel with and whom you don't. Choose your roomies wisely for sure, but *choose a roomie!* There are a lot of places where you can get a two-bedroom or a suite with a little living area that breaks it up and gives you more space, so you are not on top of each other all the time. There are always options and you can make it work if you want to. When you are back in New York sweating out your unemployment or bartending job (hopefully not!) we'll bet if you knew you could have saved an extra $10,000 while on tour, it might make sharing your space not seem so bad.

Side note about pets: We love animals and have been dog owners most of our lives. Unfortunately, they can be very costly to tour with. We know very well that pets are family members, and we wouldn't want to make the decision to either take our pet on the road or not. The reality is that it will cost you a lot more money to travel with your furry little friend. Most airlines charge extra, anywhere between $50 and $150 per flight. Also, about 75 percent of hotels charge a (often non-refundable) pet fee.

Sometimes you have to stay at the more expensive hotel offered because that is the only one that takes pets. It can be hard to find a roommate because not everyone loves living with an animal, especially in close quarters. If you are a car ride away from the hotel, you either have to bring your pet with you to the theatre (if you are allowed) or go back in between shows to let him/her out. This can be troublesome with traffic and logistics, because you are usually sharing your rental with several other cast members. We're not saying it can't be done or that it may not be worth it to have your "child" with you: we just want you to know the realities you may encounter by travelling with your pet. Again, it is doable and we have been on tours with many people who loved having their pets on the road. Just be aware it is going to be a much bigger time, money, and energy investment.

Stay with friends and family: If you are like us, you have friends, cousins, aunts, uncles and old girlfriends/boyfriends scattered across this country. If you are comfortable with it, and they are OK with it, stay with them when your tour comes through town. We have found that if friends or family know you are coming to town and have room, they will usually offer for you to stay at their place. Most likely you will have to rent a car and possibly pay for parking at the theatre, but you could also save about $400–$500 of your per diem even after you buy groceries.

Speak with your company mangers about the possibility of getting a parking pass at the theatre, because sometimes they can make that happen at a discount. Also, do your online comparison-shopping to rent your car. As we spoke about before, use your rental car company's frequent renter cards. You may qualify for complimentary upgrades and/or great deals on rentals.

> *About staying with family/friends: Part of the reason we both love being on tour is that we get to see our extended family and friends all across the country. While we all want to save money, make sure you don't allow yourself to get into an uncomfortable situation over it. For example, if they have kids, and you absolutely must sleep in every day, then it may not be a good idea to stay with them. Also, when you stay with people, there can be expectations about eating dinner with them or coming home after the show and hanging out instead of going out with the cast or doing cast activities in that city. Again, it can be a great thing to stay with friends and family, we just want you to keep all this in mind as you make your decisions.*

Summing up

A theme that seemed to come up a lot for us as we were writing this book is that the decisions you make—or don't make for that matter—will affect you down the road. That may seem a bit obvious, but we think it bears mentioning again. We just do not want anyone to look back on their financial decisions while they had a great job and say, "Oh, if only I had done this..." or, "Boy, if I had saved/invested/managed my money better in my twenties I would be in a much different place now..." You get the point. This business can be so fickle. One minute you are on Broadway living the dream and the next you are back signing up for a chorus call at the Equity building. It is just the nature of what we do. The point is that the choices you make about having a roommate on the road, taking (or not taking) a pet with you, or doing a little research and staying at a much cheaper housing option will pay you dividends for a long time.

We are not asking you to live on fast food. We like the finer things in life and definitely spend some money when we go out on date nights. We like to stay in nice hotels from time to time and we love a good meal—we're talking 5-star good meal! If you implement some of the ideas we talk about and get really good at managing your income, you will feel like you *can* go out for a really nice dinner because you'll have already budgeted for it!

For work outside New York that is not a tour, a lot of the same financial rules apply. When you work at a theatre for three weeks or more and have an apartment with a kitchen, you can save some money there. But you can also *spend* some. Buying new ketchup, mayo, and spices can add up if you aren't going to take home what's leftover. We know that may sound trite, but besides being a waste of food, it's a drag on your wallet. When you work out of town for a certain amount of time, you are usually allotted a certain amount of shipping that is paid for by the producers. Take advantage of this and send some necessities ahead of you. Once again, your bank account will thank you!

If you are staying in a hotel that offers a complimentary breakfast in the morning, get your backside out of bed and take advantage of it. Go back to bed if you need to! If you go out to a pizza joint, take what you don't eat home and stretch that out for another meal or two. Again, we are not telling you to eat like a poor college student; just see where you can easily stretch a penny without it *feeling* like you are stretching a penny.

Christine: I think one of the many pleasures in life is eating. Joe and I really enjoy eating healthy, clean food like fresh fish or a beautiful organic salad. On the flipside, you don't need to eat at high-end restaurants every day because that will add up. I remember talking with a friend who had been on the My Fair Lady *national tour with me a few months after we closed, and she lamented the fact that she had eaten out for breakfast almost every day. This can add up to roughly $10–$15 if you get eggs, coffee, orange juice, etc. She said, "If only I had eaten oatmeal in my room a few days a week, imagine the money I could have saved." (By the way, say you* **had** *eaten oatmeal and a banana in your room four days a week and saved that $40. Over a 52-week tour, that is an extra $2,080 in your pocket.)*

As a general rule, restaurants give you way too much food. As soon as it is delivered to your table, ask for a to-go box. Immediately, put half of your lunch or dinner in there. Take it back to your room for the next meal. This is not only good for your wallet, but for your waistline too! There are always many ways to trim your spending here and there and you must find a personal balance for sure. Being aware and conscious of your out-of-town spending on food is a big step in the Thriving Artists direction. Keep receipts and tally them up every week to keep yourself in check. Just because you get a tax-free per diem, does not mean you should spend it all. Believe us when we tell you, it will make things much easier when you are back to big-city life.

Chapter 10 - Taxes

"Death, taxes, and childbirth! There's never any
convenient time for any of them."
–Margaret Mitchell, Gone with the Wind

We are going to cover just a few things in this section because quite frankly, we aren't qualified to talk about taxes in detail. We will lay some groundwork for you and then it is up to you to contact a tax professional and go over your unique situation and how best to file your tax return.

There are different categories under which you can file your tax return with the IRS, but the one we would like to make you aware of is filing as a Qualified Performing Artist (QPA). According to the IRS, the criteria for being considered a QPA is the following:

1. You earn at least $200 from two different performance jobs

2. Your job-related expenses are more than 10 percent of your income from performing jobs

3. You have an adjusted gross income of $16,000 or less

4. Your filing status cannot be "married filing separately"

This category was created in 1986 and unfortunately may not apply to as many artists as it should. The reason is that the $16,000 cap on income has not adjusted with inflation. In today's dollars, that cap should be around $32,000 or more and therefore, a lot more artists would likely qualify and be able to take advantage of the deductions this category affords. Just to be clear, being a "qualified" performing artist has nothing to do with your talent! It is simply a category that was created to allow artists certain tax write-offs that people in other professions cannot.

That is really all we are going to say about this way of filing your tax return. As we said earlier you *must* speak to a tax professional *who understands working artists,* and who knows what you may deduct regardless of your QPA status.

Christine's Tax Receipt System
No matter how you are going to file, *you have to do your preparation for tax time* and that is what we will look at now.

Christine: Preparing for tax season is the one thing that I take care of almost exclusively. I don't dread April 15 in the least. Because I have done my receipt sorting, expense journaling, and pay stub filing throughout the entire year, getting all the numbers I need is a breeze. Here is a system that works for me, and perhaps it will for you, too. Feel free to take this and make it your own.

I am a paper person, like pen to paper. I don't record my receipts on Quicken® or QuickBooks® or the like, although these are perfectly good ways of categorizing and keeping track of your receipts. I do it by hand, because it is most effective for me. Also, I have learned that a handwritten log of your receipts is very credible with the IRS if you ever were to get audited (hopefully you never will). Think about it, who is going to go back and write in a whole year of receipts when the IRS comes knockin' at your door? Sure, people have done it, but I want you to avoid that sort of ulcer-causing stress as much as possible!

So first get yourself some sort of planner or ledger with lined sheets of blank paper. We have multiple businesses so I have to keep separate pages for each. Also, get at least one of those accordion envelopes to file your receipts in after you have recorded them on paper. I label each pocket: classes/lessons, medical, union, gas/parking, etc. We have three of those file folders, one for theatre and one for our side business(s).

In my ledger I make a page titled "With Receipts" and a page titled "Without Receipts." Again, I do this for both theatre and my businesses separately. Whenever I buy something, go see a show, take a dance class or buy an ink cartridge for our printer, I write down the date, amount, and what it was for on the correlating sheet of paper. *Record this information on the same day you purchased something or the next day at the latest.* This action is especially important if you didn't get a receipt for something you bought. <u>*Write it down*</u>. If you think you are going to remember it next February when you are sitting on your bed with hundreds of papers around you, think again.

After you write it down, file it in the corresponding accordion file category. Guess what? You are done! It's that simple.

If you find you can't do it every day or every other day, then have a box on your desk for your receipts. At the end of each week (or each month) you can write down and file your receipts at that time; but you had better write down those expenses that you didn't get a receipt for immediately, otherwise you won't remember and you won't get the tax benefit of that purchase.

Below is a quick sample of what my log looks like so you can use it as a guide.

SAMPLE OF CHRISTINE'S THEATRE TAX LOG

With receipt	Without receipt
1/23 - $18 dance class	2/3 – $2.25 resume copies
2/10 - $59 AEA dues	3/4 – $7.95 taxi to audition
3/10 - $100 health insurance contribution	

SAMPLE OF CHRISTINE'S BUSINESS TAX LOG

With receipt	Without receipt
1/14 - $2.95 shipping to customer X	1/24 - $25 makeup donation to BCEFA
2/4 - $50.00 website maintenance	2/7 - $5.50 copies of product ingredients sheet
3/5 - $5.59 paper for printer	

Continue to keep track like this from January 1 all the way through New Year's Eve. Then when you organize/total up for your accountant you are in *much* better shape.

Something that I have been doing for the past few years that has been working is adding up my receipts during the week between Christmas and New Year's. There are no auditions and generally I have a lot more down time. I get it done and it rocks! Of course there are still some last-minute things that come in, so

I do everything in pencil, but the lion's share of the work is over. I don't put my finished tallies on the sheet that I will give to my accountant until after the first of the year. "What sheet?" you may ask? Don't worry; we will give that to you in a moment.

Okay, so you are ready to tally up your numbers. I get a separate piece of paper that is my scratch/adding sheet and put all of my categories on it. Then it is just simple math and adding up all the totals you have under each category. So for example, you would write union dues, classes/lessons, office expenses etc. and add up all of the receipts and without receipts numbers. If you have been diligent and accurate, you can just all up all actual receipts you have in each particular category from your file folders. But you will have to go through your handwritten diary/ledger to add up all of your without receipts totals. I highlight the entry after I have added it up. I use different color highlighters so it's easier on the eyes. Then you will be able to spot the without receipts you haven't added up yet. Once you have double-checked that your amounts are correct, you enter them onto the form below.

Download and print: Thriving Artists Getting Ready for Your Tax Appointment Form www.TheThrivingArtists.com/resources.html

DISCLAIMER: We are not tax professionals or accountants. Tax laws change all the time so please rely on your tax professional to keep you up-to-date on what is happening. We are not responsible if you get audited!

You may be asking yourself what kinds of expenses and purchases you are allowed to write off on your taxes each year. The following is a list of categories that our accountant gives us the OK to take as deductions based on purchases and expenses throughout the year. Again, *consult with your own tax professional with regards to what you can and cannot deduct.*

ARTIST BUSINESS EXPENSES

Advertising, Publicity and Mailings: This is your postage for headshots and resumes to agents, casting directors, etc. This is also the expense for postcards or fliers you created to advertise your new cabaret show.

<u>Agent and Manager Fees:</u> This should be pretty easy to fill out, because if your agent's 10 percent comes directly out of your check each week, all you have to do is add it up. If it is *not* automatic and you write your agent a check each week, then just save and add up your duplicate check copies. Standard commission fees that an actor pays are 10 percent for agents and 10–15 percent for managers. If you have both, then 20–25 percent can be written off as a deduction.

<u>Dancewear, Costumes, etc</u>: Obviously any dancewear (leotards, tights, dance shoes) is deductible. If you did a show and bought a dress for it and you weren't reimbursed, that is a write-off as well. But you can't write off the shirt and tie you bought for your *Law & Order* audition. If you can wear it for personal use, it can't be written off. On the other hand, if you buy scrubs or a police uniform for TV/film work, that is 100 percent deductible.

<u>Equipment Rental</u>: This may apply to musicians who rented amps, speakers, microphones, and the like to record their CDs. A lot of actors create their own voice-over demos and have rented equipment for that.

<u>Equipment Repairs</u>: If you upgraded the memory on your computer or tuned your piano, this category is for you.

<u>Gifts (Professional only and $25 maximum per recipient/per year)</u>: These are opening/closing night gifts, holiday gifts for your agents/managers, etc. If you spent $250 on your cast for opening night, you have to itemize what you spent on each person and list all of your cast/crew.

<u>Lessons and Coaching (All)</u>: This should hopefully be a large-ish amount, because that means you are still honing and perfecting your craft! This is every dance class, voice lesson, coaching that you take.

<u>Local Transportation</u>: This is *not* commuting. You can't write off your entire monthly subway or bus card. If you keep an accurate record of your auditions, background jobs, etc., you can write off the individual subway/bus/taxi expenses you incurred.

<u>Makeup, Wigs, Hair Care (professional use only)</u>: Sometimes your makeup and hair supplies are provided, sometimes they aren't. Whatever lipstick, mascara, and blush you buy for your production of XYZ show and don't get reimbursed for

is a write-off. If the theatre provides haircuts to maintain the look of the show, and you tip $20 to the stylist, that tip is a write-off; however, getting your hair cut and colored to match your current pictures and resumes is not. *(Note: if a producer asks you to change the style of your natural hair for a show, it is on them to pay for the initial styling and to pay to have your hair returned to the way it was when you signed your contract. Read the fine print when this is being asked of you, and get everything in writing!)*

Office Expenses: This is your paper and ink for your printer, staples, paper clips, etc. Remember though this is for business use, not for your wedding invitations.

Online Services (business use only): If you have a website for your acting career, band, improv group, etc. it is a deduction. This includes the amount you bought it for in that tax year, if you pay a designer to update it, and any other ongoing fees. If you subscribe to *actors access* for the year, *Backstage*, or any of those sites for employment opportunities, they are all write-offs as well. (Oh, and don't forget about the *Theater Development Fund/Goldstar memberships too… great deals on tickets there!)

Headshots and Resumes: This could be a considerable deduction for your taxes. Christine invested a large amount of money the year she got her headshots taken. Your hair and makeup charges for headshots should be filed under the "makeup and hair care" category. The "headshot & resume" category also applies to copies of your resume for mailings and auditions. If you bought postcards, business cards, comp cards, etc. they are deductible as well.

Professional Publication and Subscriptions: If you subscribe to *Entertainment Weekly*, *Ross Reports*, *American Theatre*, *Variety*, or any publication that is related to your career, it is a deduction.

Professional Fees, Legal, Accounting (not tax prep): If you have a lawyer review a contract, or you have an accountant keeping track of your many streams of income, this is the category for you. You might leave this blank for now. Someday you will be making money from so many different sources that you will need to hire a professional to keep track of it. Sometimes you have to spend a *little* money to keep *a lot* of money. Don't be cheap here. If you are earning a significant amount of money and don't know where it is going, then it is time to hire a professional.

<u>Research Viewing (Theatre, Film, Concerts)</u>: Any film, show, concert, cabaret, live music that you see is a write-off. You are studying your craft. Movies purchased online, your Netflix subscription, and any DVDs you buy count too. Just track your research viewing with what you are currently studying, working on, or auditioning for.

<u>Research Material (Scripts, CDs, Books, Music)</u>: This includes the sheet music you bought in a store or online, the recording you bought, and all the stuff you bought on iTunes. Also don't forget about your monologue books, the biography on Cary Grant and that copy of "Our Town" that you bought from a yard sale for $1—it's all a write-off.

<u>Studio and Theatre Rental</u>: Anytime you rent a studio to warm up for an audition or coach with a teacher is a deduction.

<u>Supplies (Professional: Theatre, Touring, Dressing Room)</u>: This is often a bigger deduction when you are working out of town. When you need to buy toothpaste, floss, or towels for your makeup station, they are all a write-off.

<u>Telephone (Business use only) or Total of Phone Bills</u>: This is one for your accountant, unless you have an itemized bill and want to tally every call you make to your agent/manager or to a rehearsal space to reserve a studio. We would suggest adding up the total and taking a percentage. If you have two phones (either two cellular or one cellular and one land line) there are more deductions, but consult with your accountant on this matter.

<u>Tips (Backstage, Dressers, Stage Doormen)</u>: This one can really add up. If you are on tour and are tipping your wig people $10 a week and your personal dresser $15 a week, your total for the year is $520 for hair and $780 for dressers. That grand total is $1,300 in tips alone! Surely this is something you would want to keep track of and deduct from your taxes!

<u>Union Dues and Assessments</u>: This is another category that may make you wince at the end of the year, but it is all part of being in a professional union and making money. If you joined Actors' Equity Association this year, then you will be writing off $1,100 to join (as of this writing). If you think that is bad, wait until you join SAG-AFTRA at approximately $3,000! Equity dues are $59 paid bi-annually and all of this is a write-off as well. The Working Dues are the 2.25 percent that

comes out of your check every week while doing an Equity production and you will see this as a deduction on your pay stub. If you make the exact same amount every single week with no increases then you can take your total salary for that year, multiply it by 2.25 percent and that amount is your Working Dues for the year. Particular as we are, we went through every pay stub and added it all up. That total number is also on the W-2 that you get, so you might be able to save yourself some time and trouble.

Business Dinners, Business Entertaining: This one can get tricky. As always, you need all of your receipts for tax time, but business dinners and entertaining also need five elements of detail. These are:

1. Cost

2. Date

3. Description of meal (not just a total). For example, hamburger, Coke and cheesecake and their respective amounts.

4. Business purpose

5. Relationship with whom you ate dinner

The more detailed your receipts are, the better.

If you host a party for business purposes, 100 percent of all the food and alcohol are deductible.

There are other expenses such as healthcare premiums, childcare, mortgage interest, interest on your school loan payments, etc. Again, check with your tax professional.

*Theatre Development Fund: (www.tdf.org) The membership is $30 for the year and basically, you get tickets at half or a third of the price. You may not get the hottest show in town, but if sales are a little slow, tickets will be made available for TDF members. Check it out and support live theatre! And you don't have to wait in line at TKTS! You can order your tickets from the comfort of your own home and pick them up at the box office. To become a member of TDF you must belong to one of the following groups:

- Full-time students (high school or college/grad school)
- Full-time teachers
- Recent graduates (twenty-six years of age and under)
- Union members
- Retirees (no longer working and at least sixty-two years of age or older)
- Civil service employees
- Staff members of not-for-profit organizations
- Non-exempt employees
- Performing arts professionals
- Members of the armed forces or clergy

*Goldstar – (www.goldstar.com) is the LA online version of TDF/TKTS.

Chapter 11 - The Budget

We can't stress enough the importance of putting yourself on a budget and sticking to it. The reason to use the money management system we outlined earlier is to ultimately help you manage your money more effectively. Think of budgeting like calorie counting. Hasn't it happened that all of a sudden your jeans are tight and you have no idea how it happened? The same can be said for your savings account.

Below is a list of common expenses. Fill in your numbers and be as accurate as you can. Look at old bills and make your best estimation where you don't have a fixed expense. As you generate income use this information to keep you on track with what you spend, what you save, and what you invest.

Download and print The Thriving Artists Budget Sheet by going to www.TheThrivingArtists.com/resources.html

MONTHLY INCOME

Salary (this is net take-home pay, after taxes, 401(k), agent fees, etc.) $

MONTHLY EXPENSES
Rent/Mortgage $
Taxes on home property $
Cell phone $
Electric/Gas $
Water $
Cable/Internet $
Home phone (may be bundled with cable bill) $
Union dues $
Minimum credit card payment $
Other credit card minimums (combined or separate) $
Gym $
School loan payment $
Health insurance premiums ($33.33/month AEA) $
Laundry/Dry cleaning $
Car payment $
Car insurance $

Website expenses (webmaster/hosting) $
Subway or bus card/Transportation $
Food $
Grooming $
Misc. (clothing, drugstore, mailings, etc.) $

TOTAL MONTHLY EXPENSES $
REMAINING MONTHLY BALANCE $

EXTRA EXPENSES (Necessary, but could be cut if
money is super tight)
Voice lessons/Coaching $
Acting classes $
Dance class $
Yoga/Pilates $
Massage/Acupuncture/Body work $
Theatre/Concerts/Movies $

TOTAL MONTHLY EXPENSES (with extras) $

REMAINING MONTHLY BALANCE $

Now do the math. Monthly income – your expenses (with/with out extras) =
your balance.

If you can stick to those numbers and keep yourself running with a positive balance, you are winning the game. If the ends are not meeting like you want them
to you have two options; either figure out a way to generate more income, or cut
spending. This exercise is designed to hold up a mirror to your day-in and day-
out financial life. If it scares you, that is fine, *fill in the numbers anyway*. You can't
get where you want to go if you don't know where you are.

When you are on the road it is a great idea to live and cover all your expenses
exclusively from your per diem. Take a look at the following section and when
you are on the road, put your numbers in and see what exactly is happening in
your financial world as you travel about! Being on tour is the best place to save
and invest a lot of money, *but it doesn't happen without you taking action*!

Total weekly per diem amount $

WEEKLY LIVING EXPENSES ON TOUR
Rent/Hotel for the week (inc. taxes) $
Rental car (weekly rental rate) $
Food (total of *all* food/drink for the week) $
Gas $
Parking $
Tolls $
Laundry/Dry cleaning $
Gym fee/Pilates/Yoga/Dance classes/Massage $
Tips to maids, bellhops $
Tips to dressers/hair $
Extras (toothpaste/drugstore/clothes) $
Misc. (sightseeing/movies/entertainment) $
Health insurance premiums ($33.33/month AEA) $
Gifts (going away/birthdays) $
Other travel expenses (overweight baggage/pet fees) $
Cell phone $

TOTAL MONTHLY EXPENSES $

EXTRA EXPENSES (calculate weekly)
Apartment back home (hopefully you can sublet it), storage unit, car payment, etc. $

BALANCE OF WEEKLY PER DIEM $

Do the same math once again:
Weekly per diem – expenses (with/without extras) = weekly balance

This budget sheet is to ensure that your living expenses on tour do not exceed what you are allotted for per diem. If you are carrying some extra expenses such as rent back in your home city, a car payment and/or insurance, etc., do your best not to exceed your per diem, but if you do go over, work to dip into your salary *only* for those extra expenses. If you aren't carrying extra expenses or only minimal ones, you will hopefully be able to save some of your per diem money every week. Having an extra $100-$200 a week to actively manage (save/invest) really adds up.

TRACKING YOUR NET WORTH

This is an activity that is more revealing than anything we have ever done. At the beginning of every month we take a look at all of our assets versus our liabilities and come up with our current net worth. Keeping with the philosophy that what you focus on expands, we love focusing energy on this activity because 95 percent of the time our net worth has gone up rather than down...and we have been doing this since June 2007!

Download and print: The Thriving Artists Net Worth Tracking Sheet www. TheThrivingArtists.com/resources.html Make copies, enter your numbers every month, and see what happens!

THE NET WORTH TRACKING SHEET PART 1 – YOUR ASSETS

CASH and LIQUID ASSETS

Cash and Bank Accounts – This is every checking, savings, CDs, Emigrant Direct, Capitol360 account that you have. The money you have under the mattress or in the icebox counts too! (Don't forget to include the money you have in your wallet.)

Money owed to you – Self-explanatory. If your brother Bob owes you $500, that counts. Add it up!

MARKET ASSETS

Mutual Funds –All the money you have invested with Charles Schwab, T Rowe Price, Fidelity, Roth IRAs, etc.

Stocks – Your Ameritrade account, E-Trade, ShareBuilder, or any account where you are buying and selling individual stocks yourself. This is where you enter how much money you have in individual stocks. Your mutual funds may be invested in the stock market, but those numbers go into the mutual funds category. These are individual stocks that you own currently like Starbucks or Apple. Virtually every account has a viewing feature where you can see your account gain/loss amounts. Take the current value of your stock portfolio and enter it into your Net Worth Tracking Sheet.

FIXED ASSETS

Real Estate Investments – This is not your personal or second home. This is for investment properties only. If you own an apartment building, an empty lot, parking garage, or a house you rent out, here is where you record those numbers.

Other – Any other fixed asset we have not mentioned.

LONG-TERM ASSETS

Retirement Savings Plan – This is any 401(k) that you have. These are usually investments that are tied to a company or your job. If you are in AEA, hopefully you have taken advantage of the 401(k) plan whenever you could, and have money in there. If you work a "day job" at a company that provides a 401(k), be sure to include all those numbers here as well.

Cash Value of Whole Life Insurance – Many of you may not have a life insurance plan yet. Christine wouldn't either except her grandfather bought all of his grandchildren a policy when they were very young. Whole life insurance policies have a cash value attached to it and if so, that value will be on your statement. You could cash out your plan for that amount at any time if you desperately needed the money. However we wouldn't recommend it except in an extreme emergency.

Pension Plans – Thankfully, if you are in a union (AEA, SAG-AFTRA) and have worked union jobs, you have a pension plan. You will get these statements at the end of the year that will tell you how much is in your pension fund. We love looking at these, because it's like an extra account that has been set up for you for retirement and you often forget about it.

Other – If one of your long-term assets doesn't fit into one of the above categories.

PERSONAL ASSETS

Personal Residence –Here is where you get to write down what your house or apartment is worth. If you get it appraised, make sure you write down the most recent number. Note: Previously we spoke about the merits of renting, however to be clear, owning a home is a great thing…*when you can afford it.* However, this section is not to argue the benefits/drawbacks of owning your home, but to calculate your net worth. If you own your home, it is a crucial part of calculating your net worth.

Recreational Property – If you own a second home or a beach property that isn't a rental, this is the category to list it in.

Vehicles – How much are your vehicle(s) worth? This can be your car(s), motorcycle(s), etc. These you may have to look up online or if you have a smart-phone, just download the app "Black Book iUsedCar" for (currently) $1.99. It gives you a very accurate idea of what your car is worth based on certain criteria. There are several apps out there that do similar calculations, but we know that particular one is good. By now it is conventional wisdom that as soon as a new car is driven off the lot, it can decrease 15 to 20 percent in value in the first year alone. If you were to sell your car right now, what could you realistically get for it? That is the number to use.

Recreational Equipment - If you are a snowmobiler or avid skier, how much is all your gear worth? Again, look it up as best you can. If you sell this equipment and get less than you have been recording every month, you might be disappointed when your net worth goes down.

Household Furnishings and Equipment - When we do this, we add up our nice furniture that we could sell, our computers, and all our electronic equipment. We don't get too bogged down in this category. We have a number and unless we buy new furniture or some crazy hot new sound system, that number stays where it is for the most part. Over time it gradually decreases due to depreciation (same as a car losing its value).

Collectibles (stamps, coins, jewelry) – This is self-explanatory. If you have a coin collection, how much is it worth? You can also count any gold, silver, or other precious metal coins/bars that you have invested in as well. Look up the value on any market index and you'll see what it is worth at the time.

Artwork - If you own any, add it up and write it down.

Other – You get the idea. Anything that has monetary value, add it up and write it here.

THE NET WORTH TRACKING SHEET PART 2 – YOUR DEBT

SHORT-TERM DEBT
<u>Charge Accounts and Credit Cards</u> – This is the total of all the balances on your credit card(s).

<u>Line of Credit</u> – This is from your personal or business bank account, or that you would have in a HELOC (home equity line of credit). (You don't have to enter a number here if you have not taken out any money on a line of credit).

<u>Loans</u> (car, student) – How much do you owe on your car? How much for your school loan?

<u>Unpaid Bills</u> – If you have let your electric bill go for the month you are in, be honest and write it down. You are not doing yourself any favors by leaving it off this sheet. Putting information like that on paper can spur you into action.

<u>Taxes</u> (income or property tax owing) – If you owe money to the IRS or your state government, write it down. *And then pay it off as soon as you can.*

<u>Other</u> (family obligations, charity pledges)

LONG-TERM DEBT
<u>Home Mortgage</u> – How much do you still owe on your home?

<u>Other Mortgage Loans</u> - If you still owe on your rental or investment properties and carry a mortgage, write that here. If you are responsible for a family member's home, write it down here as well.

<u>Other</u> – This is any other long-term debt that you may have.

Once again it is a case of simple math. Add up all your assets, and then subtract from that all your debts. What you are left with is your true net worth. We have found over the years is that sometimes you are cash-rich and investment poor, or you can be cash-poor and your investments could be going through the roof. In the best of times they are *both* going up! Either way, if you see your monthly total heading north, then you are doing the right things. This practice also can put you in a "wealth" mindset rather than an "income" mindset. Yes, income is important, but you generally won't hear about the crazy rich people such as Mark Zuckerberg, Bill Gates, and Oprah Winfrey being talked about for how much they make; people talk about how much they are *worth*. It may seem subtle, but it can be a powerful shift in your thinking, because you can make millions of dollars yet have a negative net worth if you spend more than you take in. So don't be awed by someone's paycheck; be awed by his or her ability to manage that paycheck and have a growing net worth!

Chapter 12 - To College or Not to College

> "I think everyone should go to college and get a degree
> and then spend six months as a bartender and six months
> as a cabdriver. Then they would really be educated."
> ### - Al McGuire

Countless times we have been asked by aspiring performers in high school, "Should I go to college, or should I move straight to the city?" There is no "right" answer to this question. We have both seen young performers who move straight to New York and land a Broadway show within months. We have also seen artists go to a great college, graduate and then book a big national tour. They wouldn't trade those college years for anything.

We both went to four-year colleges/universities. Joe received a BFA in Musical Theatre from Penn State University and Christine went to DeSales University (formerly Allentown College) and holds a BA in Theatre.

Neither one of us would give up those wonderful years. We made lifelong friends and because of those relationships now have extensive networks both in New York and Los Angeles. Like we said, there is no "right" answer, just what is right for you.

Joe: I went to a school with a great musical theatre program (Penn State), because I knew that's exactly what I needed. I was an athlete growing up, rather than a dancer, and I had only just started taking voice lessons halfway through my junior year of high school. The fact that Penn State offered all of this training, that the facilities and faculty were exactly what I wanted, and it was an in-state school (wasn't going to break the bank) all made PSU a great fit for me. Also, they had a conservatory approach while in a traditional college setting and I loved having both worlds at my fingertips. Ultimately what you put into college is what you are going to get out of it. I knew that wherever I went, I was going to focus and work exceptionally hard to get absolutely everything out of the program. I squeezed every ounce of experience, training, knowledge that I could out of it. Two things that came of this experience were 1. I graduated very prepared artistically, and 2. I graduated without six figures of debt.

Christine: I had a good deal of performing experience by the time I reached high school. I started dancing at age seven and performing in musicals at age twelve. When I was fourteen, I was already dancing at Broadway Dance Center in New York City. Could I have moved to New York right after high school? Probably. Would I have booked a performing job? Maybe. Would I have had a nervous breakdown? Very likely! I'm from a medium-sized city, Harrisburg, Pennsylvania, and I needed more nurturing. I chose DeSales because I saw the play Harvey *on their main stage. I was completely blown away by their production values, the actors' level of expertise, and the facilities. I looked at about five other schools and probably would have been happy there too, but I am glad I chose DeSales. It was a small program (about twenty people in my freshman class) and there were big advantages to this. We didn't have a graduate degree program so all the shows are cast with undergrads. We got to do* Death of a Salesman *and* Sweeney Todd *and actually play the lead roles. The experience I garnered was invaluable. The beauty of where I went to college is its proximity to New York City. It's about an hour and a half drive away from DeSales University, and by my senior year, I was either driving in or taking the bus to hit auditions at least once a week. It was a great way to marry what I was learning in school and directly apply it to the real world. I wouldn't trade those four years for anything.*

You certainly don't need a four-year degree to be a Thriving Artist. Below is an interview with Cameron Adams. She is an extraordinary performer who has had *major* success in New York. She recently was an original cast member and understudy to Rosemary in the revival of *How to Succeed in Business Without Really Trying* starring Daniel Radcliffe, and then moved on to yet another high-profile job, *Nice Work If You Can Get It* starring Matthew Broderick. She was in the ensemble and understudies the female star, Kellie O'Hara. Her other Broadway credits include: *Promises, Promises, The Music Man* as Zaneeta (and in the movie with Matthew Broderick), *Oklahoma!*, *Hairspray*, *Cry Baby*, and *Shrek the Musical* just to name a few. She is an example of someone who, while still in her teens, moved to New York shortly after high school and is making huge things happen. Here is what Cameron had to say to us:

INTERVIEW WITH CAMERON ADAMS

When did you start dancing?

I started around four years old.

What was your first show and how old were you?

My first professional show was *The Music Man* and I was seventeen years old. I didn't do a ton of community theatre growing up, because there wasn't very much of it in my hometown. But I think my first community theatre gig was called *Snow White and the Seven Surfers* and it was performed at the First Presbyterian Church in Myrtle Beach, South Carolina.

How old were you when you moved to New York?

I was seventeen years old and halfway through my junior year of high school.

Did you consider going to college?

I was just starting to look at different schools when I auditioned for *The Music Man* and I was for sure not going to move to NYC right away. I knew I wanted to go to college and do the normal route. When I got the job it was a shock and a huge change for everyone. We were not a showbiz family and I was not a theatre kid.

What colleges did you look at?

I hadn't really decided yet. I was still pretty young, so I was just starting to think about what kind of school I would want to go to.

What did your parents think about your decision to move to New York at such a young age?

They were amazing! It was not an easy transition because I was so close to being eighteen and ready to be on my own, but at the same time I was still in high school and for sure not ready to move to NYC by myself. My mom was a dance teacher and she helped me get adjusted to the North by coming up with me for the first ten months that I lived up here. My parents are still happily married, so that was not easy for them. Also, I had an older brother in college at the time. My dad flew up a good bit and once I got comfortable after about a month or so, my mom flew home a lot for weekends and stuff. It was not an easy time for any of us and a huge, huge adjustment for our family.

Where did you live?

I lived in a pre-furnished apartment on the Upper West Side, 71st between Columbus and Central Park West. We had no furniture with us so we had to find a place that already had a bed in it. Haha! Also, I wasn't sure if I was going to stay up here that long or if the show was going to run very long. There was always an understanding that if I wasn't happy or the show closed early, that I would go to college.

What was your first audition here?

I think it was a commercial, but I can't remember what for.

How did it go?

I was terrible. Had no clue what the hell I was doing.

Talk about the experience of working on *The Music Man* and what you learned.

It was great moving up here with a job, but it was such a growing two years for me. I started the show at seventeen and when we closed I was nineteen! Those years are full of growing and changing and it was definitely strange doing it up here. I met some amazing people who are still a part of my life and I also worked with incredible people who have helped open other doors. I would not trade my experience for anything else.

If you could do it again, would you still make the same decisions?

Absolutely! They may not have been easy, but this was my journey and my experience! This was my personal road, even if it was different than someone else's.

What would you say to a young performer contemplating going to college or moving right away to a big city?

I always say college is a great route, because you can get different degrees and also I think you make lifelong friends and have amazing experiences that you could never have anywhere else. But if you feel like NYC (or any big city) is the place for you right away, and you're ready to work hard and put yourself out there, then go for it!

Wouldn't it be great if every artist's story were like that?

Christine: I sometimes wonder what would have happened if I had moved to New York right away. I do think I would have booked work. Where I think I would have been blown out of the water in an audition was in my acting while singing. I had no clue how to make song lyrics come to life. The idea of using lyrics as a monologue was completely foreign to me. If this is sounding like Greek to you right now then run, don't walk, to a musical theater acting class.

Our next interview is with Kirsten Scott. Her first Broadway show was *Hairspray* after graduating from Carnegie Mellon University. Kirsten has since gone on to work in top regional theaters with original shows like *Minsky's* and *Limelight: The Story of Charlie Chaplin*. She also played Young Phyllis in *Follies* on Broadway, and is currently originating the new Broadway musical, *Big Fish* with renowned director/choreographer, Susan Stroman. Kirsten is a shining example of someone who went to college, got a degree, and then started working as a full time professional actor. This is what Kirsten had to share with us:

INTERVIEW WITH KIRSTEN SCOTT

When did you start dancing/performing?
I started taking dance classes when I was five, and broke into theater at the age of thirteen.

What was your first show and how old were you?
My first show was the *Wizard of Oz*, when I was thirteen. I played a man, the Emerald City Guard, and I was in the Lullaby League.

What colleges did you look at?
I looked at CMU (Carnegie Mellon University), CCM (Cincinnati Conservatory of Music), Michigan, Juilliard, Point Park, Syracuse, Ithaca, and Penn State.

Did you consider moving right to New York?
I was in callbacks for *Hairspray* during my senior year of high school, and if I got it, I would've moved right away. But I was pretty sure I needed to go to school.

Talk about your college experience.

I loved it. First of all, I needed the four years to grow up, not to mention learn about myself as a person. The lessons I learned from my professors, but most of all from my fellow classmates, helped to shape the person and the actor I am today. I learned so much by spending four years absorbing everything I could from conservatory training. I respect and understand all aspects of theater, and was exposed to so many experiences I would have never had in New York. I felt safe to try things and fail, a lot. If I had known what CMU was like, I would have never considered missing out on college and going right to New York. New York wasn't as scary as it could've been when I moved here, because I had the safety net of all my classmates, and we moved here as a group. We still continue to help each other out and it's so nice to have a family in an unfamiliar city. College rocks!

Did you audition while in college? How did you fare?

Yes, I auditioned for summer stock every year. I also went to one callback for *Hairspray* my freshman year of college and was offered the role…the same role I then booked right out of college. However, I turned it down to stay in school and decided that I would only audition for summer stock until I graduated. From my summer stock auditions I worked for four years consecutively at West Virginia Public Theater, and slowly moved up in the company from ensemble to principal.

What did your parents think about your decision to go to college?

My parents were very proud of my decision to go to school, and even more proud that I got into CMU, my top choice and my father's alma mater.

Would they have supported your moving right to New York?

When I was in callbacks for *Hairspray* and offered it, my parents were completely supportive of any decision I made. They left it completely up to me and said they would be happy with whatever I decided.

How old were you when you moved to New York?

I moved to New York when I was twenty-two.

Where did you live and did you have a survival job?

When I moved to New York I first lived on 55th Street between 8th and 9th Avenues, I did not have a survival job, and am I very lucky to say that I have not had one yet.

What was your first audition here?

Technically my first audition in New York was the open call I went to for *Hairspray*. But since graduating and moving here, it was the TV show *Damages* and the musical *Cry Baby*.

How did it go?

Damages went really well. I felt confident and read well. However, for *Cry Baby*, I felt like a mess. I was a bit too nervous.

How long did you live in New York before you landed *Hairspray*?

I was in New York for about four months before I landed *Hairspray*.

Talk about that experience and what you have learned so far

Being in my first Broadway show was a dream come true. I did however feel a little green when I first started. Luckily I had the vocabulary and the training from CMU to take with me into the rehearsal room, but there's so much that you can only learn by actually doing a show on Broadway. I do feel that CMU gave me everything that a college could; you can only really learn how to do eight shows a week by actually experiencing it for yourself. The biggest lesson I have had to teach myself is pacing myself for an eight-show week. At school and in summer stock I never did a run that lasted longer than a couple weeks and because of that, it was easy to keep a show fresh and alive, and keep your endurance up. However when choreography and blocking become second nature to the point that you can do it in your sleep, you need to really make sure you are still treating everything as if it's happening for the first time. That has been the trickiest thing to learn.

If you could do it again, would you still make the same decisions?

Yes, I would not give up the time I spent and what I learned at CMU for the world!

If you had moved right to the city after high school, how do you think you would have fared?

I think I would have been OK, not great, but OK. I would have made friends, but not had the family I have now. I don't think I would have the ability or the skills to be a versatile actor and would have probably had a very different career.

As you can see from both Cameron and Kirsten, there are strong arguments for both sides.

We are sure that your family also has influential opinions one way or the other. Parents we have encountered are usually very pro-college. They feel that you should have an education to "fall back on." They are not necessarily wrong. We will refrain from supporting one side or the other because the decision is 100 percent up to you. We do, however, want to educate you on all the options, so that you can make a well-informed decision. Half of the artists out there may highly recommend going to college and the other half may say the exact opposite. We are firm believers that your journey is *your journey*. You can't hold yourself up to other people's experiences or standards. *Trust your path*. Some people know exactly what they want to do with their lives. Other people don't know what they want to major in until they are juniors in college. It's all right, just be true to yourself. If the star of your high school drama program is going to Juilliard, it doesn't mean that she will work once she has that degree. Sometimes quite the opposite can happen. We have found that often the people who were *always* cast as leads in high school or college often do not have as much success in the real world as the people who had not been the go-to casting choices for starring roles. *Not always getting what you want can be a good test of character.* It makes you answer the question, "How bad do you want it?"

Christine: When I got out into the real world, I had a good amount of success getting cast right away. Never once did I have the lead in a musical in college. I was always featured, but usually understudied the starring role. My first few jobs out of college were The Radio City Christmas Spectacular, *the national tour of* Meet Me in St. Louis, *and the European tour of* 42nd Street *playing the lead, Peggy Sawyer.*

Joe: I had to claw my way into the program at PSU, where I was rejected twice before finally getting in. After working my butt off going through the training, I eventually became the first graduate of the BFA Musical Theatre program to make it to Broadway. I don't know if it would have happened that way, or that I would have worked as tirelessly as I did, if I had not needed to fight so hard for it at the beginning. I had to come face-to-face with the question we posed before: "How bad do you want it?" Because of that experience, I found my answer. So no matter what does or doesn't happen with college, you can make the very best of it and use your experience to move you closer to your goal.

Our examples obviously do not mean that if you do land some lead roles in high school and college that you won't work in the real world. The longer we are in this business, the more we see that perseverance and character will drive your career further than talent alone ever could. Going to college or going to the "school of life" will teach you that lesson for sure. Your character, how you present yourself at auditions, in class, during rehearsals, and throughout a run of a show, will shape how you are thought of as an artist more than you can possibly know.

THE FINANCES OF COLLEGE
If you have decided that college is for you, *please do not get yourself into crazy amounts of debt.*

We know that these next few statements may not be favorable with some people but we have to say them. This book is to help you be a Thriving Artist, and how on earth can you be thriving artistically *and financially* if you are $100,000 or more in debt before you ever even get to the city, wherever that may be?

What's the answer? Some of you may be lucky enough to have parents/grandparents who can easily afford upwards of $50,000 a year for tuition. That's awesome. Some of you may qualify for academic, theatre, dance (insert your art form here) scholarships that pay for your entire time at school. That's awesome, too! Others will have to take out some loans to make college a reality. Even if you go to a state school, a lot of parents today just can't afford to pay $15,000 to $25,000 per year for tuition. The point is that you really need to look at what school costs, how far in debt you are going to be when you get out of school, and not get tunnel vision on only going to one place, because you feel they have *that* much better of a program.

Joe and Christine: We're going let you in on a little secret: The program you go to has very little to do with how successful you are going to be upon graduation. What you put into it is what you will get out of it, and there is no "magic bullet" of a school that guarantees your success. Only YOU can do that with your talent and your work ethic and all the other things we have previously talked about in this book. Please do not be sold by celebrity alumni lists. Look at the quality of the training, look at the price tag, and make your decision from there. You shape your college experience just as much as where you go shapes you. Remember that and choose wisely. Broadway pays the same whether you are debt free from your state school, or $100,000 in the hole from some other school with a prestigious name.

If you are one of the lucky ones whose parents could send you to any school you wanted, maybe you could strike a deal: What if you went to a less expensive school? Then they could put the rest of the money they would have spent on college tuition into an investment for you. Then, while you are training and stretching your skills for the next four years, your bank account is doing the same thing.

Christine: My dad lost his job the summer between my freshman and sophomore years of college. Luckily, I had received a good amount in scholarships (both academic and theatre/dance), but it didn't quite cover everything. I took out federal loans that were approximately $4,000 - $5,000 a year. You get a six-month grace period after graduation before you have to start paying, and then the bills start showing up at your doorstep every month like clockwork. If you don't want to ruin your credit, pay them. I certainly didn't want to ruin my credit or have someone knocking at my door for my payments, so I got on it immediately. Paying my school loan back every month really taught me how to manage my money and appreciate the value of making money, even more than I already did. If I could have been one of the lucky ones who came out of school debt free, would I have wanted that? You betcha! No question about it. This isn't about the merits of paying off debt, it's simply about making smart decisions and being responsible with your finances at any age...and it is never too early to start.

Joe: The way my family worked out college was that I had to pay my first year in full by myself. Typically if you are going to party too much and flunk out of school it's going to be in the first year. So my father cut the deal that if I paid my own way and did well my first year, he would pick up the rest because he would see that I was serious about my education. I think it was a brilliant way of doing it, because now that I am a parent, why would I waste money on an education my kid is just going to party his way out of? Smart thinking, Dad! Thanks!

So what's the answer? Once again, there is no clear-cut answer. We want you to follow your dreams. If you can *only* see yourself at NYU and know you won't be happy anywhere else, so be it. We have a feeling though that if you open yourself up to other possibilities, other viable options will present themselves to you. Educate yourself, look at several schools, and do your homework. We both firmly believe that everything in life is about what you put into it. The same is true for your education.

Start playing the money game now. *It's never too soon.* You will be so far ahead of your peers that you will look back in a few short years and be glad you did a little extra work now. There is no time like the present to be smart with your money.

Closing Thoughts

Our closing thoughts are really just the beginning...of *your* story. Our intention throughout this book was to give you the tools to springboard into a fulfilling and empowered journey of being a Thriving Artist. You can only construct a building as high as the foundation will allow. Take these tools, dig a huge foundation, and create your own *thriving* success story.

> "Somebody should tell us, right at the start of our lives, that we are dying. Then we might live life to the limit, every minute of every day. Do it! I say. Whatever you want to do, do it now. There are only so many tomorrows."
> **- Michael Landon**

Keep learning, keep growing...keep *Thriving*! We believe in you, and we are with you all the way.

To your success,
Joe, Christine, & The Thriving Artists Team

PS: Please stay in touch with as you continue on your adventure! Let us know how this book helped you, and if you would like us to come do a workshop in your area! Find us at www.TheThrivingArtists.com. We can't wait to hear from you!

ABOUT THE AUTHORS:

Joe Abraham and Christine Negherbon created *The Thriving Artists* as a labor of love and have since been joyously leading seminars all over the United States to teach artists about the power of being a *Thriving Artist*. With over 32 years (and counting) combined experience in show business, their careers currently span both the east and west coasts including two Broadway shows, nine National Tours, one International Tour, ten top regional theatres, numerous commercials, and working on top network television shows. Their knowledge of what it takes to 'make it' is incredibly vast, and continues to grow. They are known for leading dynamic, heartfelt, and inspiring workshops for artists all over the world. To contact, or for more detailed information on both Joe and Christine please go to <u>www.TheThrivingArtists.com</u>